SW

Walki
Värmland

THE LAKE REGION OF CENTRAL SWEDEN

Paul van Bodengraven & Marco Barten

INDEX

page

Introduction

Walking in Värmland

the walks   **distance • time • difficulty**

3

Introduction

So green, so vast and so empty. That is the feeling you will experience each time you enjoy Swedish nature. So much land and so few people is something most European countries do not have anymore. The majority of Swedish people live in the southern part of the country, which of course has everything to do with the fact that the days are longer here. In the north of the country the days are much shorter. So the further north you go, the fewer people you will encounter.

Värmland is situated approximately halfway, just north of the Oslo – Stockholm line and with so few people nature can run its own course. Värmland is a rural province, even for Swedish standards. Countryside, for Stockholm standards. Agricultural too, but in an industry that is less obvious for Western Europe: forestry. Indeed huge areas of land are used for commercial wood production.
All this greenery alternates with lots of water. Every valley has a river and behind every hill is a lake. From extremely large to charmingly small, everywhere in the province you will find water.
The Värmlanders live their lives outside and their work mostly involves nature in some way and of course they live in rural areas. They work for example as foresters or as hosts or hostesses in the outdoor sports industry. From moose safaris to rafting, from all possible alpine sports to canoeing, it's all possible here.

So much space, so much nature, so outdoor-minded, so therefore lots of possibilities for walking tours? Well, there is a bit of a disappointment here. Yes, there is certainly no lack of space, but the problem is a lack of clearly described walking tours. There are long distance paths, varying in length between 40 to 550 km; but these are all walks from A, via B and C, to Z. As a tourist you can therefore only walk back and fourth.
There are shorter walks but these are not easy to find and you have to have good knowledge of the Swedish language in order to understand where exactly you can find them. However, what is perhaps an even greater drawback is the fact that: nowhere is it written down how you should walk, the level of difficulty, what problems you may encounter and how long it will take to reach your destination. Most routes are marked, but

that is about it. The rest you will have to find out for yourself.
We want to change all this with this guide and so we have searched for the best and most beautiful walks, spread out across the province. Walks vary in length from 5.5 to over 20 km, so that there is something for everyone. The walks are all existing routes, mostly marked but which have not been plotted by us. We did, however, walk, assess and describe them and we have also visualized and mapped them. All you have to do is put on your walking boots and discover the beauty of Värmland.

GENERAL

According to the information provided by Visit Värmland, there are 11,118 lakes in the province. Lake Vänern, the biggest lake of North-western Europe, is one of these lakes. Just over 322,000 people live in Värmland, over 25% of them in Karlstad. With an area of 19,204 km², Värmland is a little smaller than South West England. To give you an idea of the space here: Värmland has, on average, 17 people per km², in South West England this is 210.

The 'green heart of Central Sweden' attracts quite a lot of tourists. Most European visitors go to the southern provinces, but those who travel further north mostly go to Värmland and neighbouring Dalarna. Interestingly, in Sweden the following applies: the further north you go, the more space there is. Most tourists visiting the province come from neighbouring countries such as Norway and Denmark, from Germany and from Sweden itself. Tourism is an increasingly important source of income, besides the more traditional industries such as forestry and agriculture.

HISTORY

When thinking of the history of Sweden, you will undoubtedly think about the Norsemen and Vikings. Until the year 1000 they ruled Scandinavia. The rise of Christianity in Scandinavia led to the formation of the forerunners of the four countries Norway, Sweden, Finland and Denmark. This does not mean that these countries always had the same shape or surface. Lots of battles were fought before the present borders came into being. For example, between 1353 and 1523 Denmark, Sweden and Norway formed the Kalmar Union; but, the Danes and Swedes did not get on particularly well and therefore lots of wars were fought during the existence of the Union. Therefore, in 1523 King Gustav I declared the unilateral independence of Sweden. Norway did the same in 1814.

However, Finnish territory was part of the Swedish kingdom until 1809 and after this period it was annexed by the Russians; until finally Finland declared independence in 1917. The fact that Finland and Sweden formed a kingdom for so long can still be seen in many ways in Swedish culture today, especially in Värmland. It is in this region, near the Norwegian border, that the nomadic Finnish

tribes settled around 1700. The forests in this region had been uninhabited until this point and these Finnish tribes lived from what the land had to offer them. The technique they used for this is described beautifully in English as 'Slash & Burn'. What it comes down to is that they would burn down a stretch of forest in order to grow crops there the following year and once the ground had been depleted, the nomads would move on. As the area is so distant and quiet, the tribes set up their 'own' free state in the Swedish-Norwegian border region. People spoke Finnish and developed their own culture and this is still clearly visible in the 21st century, for example in the architecture of some farms. For example, walk 3 goes past the Ritamäki farm, one of the best preserved farms from this era. Interestingly until well into the 20th century, people in Värmland mostly spoke Finnish and this language can also be found in the names of many villages, rivers and swamps.

Today the descendants of the Finnish people have now 'merged into' what we call Swedes and Norwegians, but the memory of these times is kept alive in many different ways. For example, the region is called 'Finnskogen' (Skog = forest : Forest of the Fins). Torsby has a wonderful museum about Finnish habitation and culture, which played such an important role in this region.

FORESTRY

Historically, money was earned in the forestry and mining industries in this region. The latter industry existed until the beginning of the 20th century, but forestry is still an important source of income today. The vast hills and the water provide good soil for the innumerable pine trees that you can find here, but most of the forests are not natural but afforested. A plot of forest needs approximately 20 years of growing before the 'harvest'. This happens in a very methodical and organised manner: an indicated hectare is cleared, while the surrounding stretches of forest remain and in this way erosion is prevented. Within three years the cleared stretch of forest is afforested again. Transportation of the cut down trees used to happen via the Klarälven, the river that cuts through the province from north to south and then discharges into the Vänern near Karlstad. The tree trunks were thrown in the water and floated with the stream down south, where they were processed. Various sawmills were and are located along the river. However, since 1991 all transportation of wood takes place by road and the only tree trunks that you can still see on the river, are those of the

rafts with which tourists go down Kläralven river. During the walking tours described in this book, you will certainly come across several stretches of cleared forest; as well as parts of forest that had not been cleared yet when we were there, and parts that have been afforested in the meantime. It can make walking difficult, but the foresters almost always leave the tree stumps untouched on which the markings can be seen. This way it is still possible to follow the route.

CLIMATE/WEATHER

The weather in Sweden is determined by what meteorologists call a 'continental climate'; which means in general that the weather is fairly stable. The average temperature in June, July and August is one degree higher than in most western European countries, despite it being Sweden's northern location. The number of solar hours is significantly higher and the number of rainy days in these summer months is also far less. Most precipitation falls during winter, when it is a lot colder, in the form of snow. The line of guaranteed snow and not guaranteed snow runs straight through Värmland, somewhere between Sunne and Torsby. The area north of Torsby is one of the most popular alpine sports destinations with Swedish people; and alpine sports resorts like Branäs, Hovfjället and Långberget have also become increasingly popular with foreigners.

FLORA

Spruce and pine trees are the most common trees in Sweden. No matter how far you look, the green hills seem endless and covered with coniferous trees; but there are differences. The trees are part of the family of conifers which is the collective name for more than 600 subspecies. The name 'Christmas tree' does not do any justice to the great diversity of coniferous trees that Värmland has. You will not come across many deciduous forests in this region. The trees that you can see most during our walks are birches, as these trees do extremely well in the damp peat areas. Oaks and beeches are less common, as they are less likely to survive the often low temperatures during the severe winters.

It would be impossible to provide a full list of all the wild flowers that you can see here in the spring and illustrations of some of the most beautiful ones have been included in this book. We have done this specifical-

ly to take away the preconception that Sweden merely consists of pine forests. To give you an idea: in the whole of Sweden you can find no less than 47 sorts of orchids of which a great many are in this region. Swedish bookstores sell several books and guides in which the various sorts are described (unfortunately almost only in the Swedish language).

A special mention should be made to the currant bushes which bear fruit in late summer and early autumn; of which the most common is the lingon or cowberry. These can be picked and eaten by everyone. However, cranberries, blueberries and other fruits can also be seen during these walks.

FAUNA

Being thinly populated the region is very attractive for many animals that can survive the cold winters. Besides common animals such as rabbits, badgers, squirrels, beavers and deer, the vast forests are also the home of moose (see below), wolves and even brown bears. You will not often come across a brown bear during our walks. In fact you will perhaps only see their footprints, as these animals are extremely shy and mostly live in places that humans cannot reach. They often move around at night in places that are not visible to the human eye.

There is an ongoing discussion in Sweden about the question whether the bear and wolf populations are too big or too small, in order to come to a proper balance between humans and animals. Some people advocate greater numbers of these animals, while others want to decrease the population by giving out more hunting permits. Whatever the truth may be, we have never come across any bears or wolves during our walks.

There is also plenty to do both alongside and on the water. For example,Värmland is a favourite fishing destination and another popular pastime is the beaver safari during which you go searching for these industrious animals via canoe and with a guide. During the walks you can often see what the beaver is capable of with its powerful teeth. There are also a great number of birds in the region with many common species such as wagtails, finches, tits, woodpeckers, blackbirds and pigeons. The bookstores in Sweden sell specialized guides in which the various species are shown and described (again unfortunately almost only in Swedish).

MOOSE AND HUNTING

The moose, the unofficial mascot of Sweden, pops up everywhere: on tea towels, coffee mugs or as key rings. In real life, however, you will not come across this huge inhabitant of the forest so easily. Moose are extremely shy and their greyish-brown colour provides excellent camouflage. Moose have excellent hearing and sense of smell, so they will almost always see you before you see them. The best chance of seeing a moose is from your car, at dusk.

Each year there are a great many moose sightings in Värmland, but the province also has the highest rate of shootings than any other in Sweden. Most moose live in central and north Värmland and in general it can be said that the less people, the more moose there are. The quietness, the space, the vast forests and the many lakes constitute the perfect habitat for these animals. Estimations of the size of the population vary from 240,000 to 300,000 and when the winter has been mild, the number of moose can be even greater.

Each year, the government allows one third of the population of moose to be killed during the hunting season; which always occurs during two weeks in October and the following weekends. During the hunt, forests are closed so you cannot walk there; so if you have plans of going to Värmland in this period, make sure to find out beforehand whether your route is accessible.

There are strict rules for the hunters. Every region gets indicated a quota. Every animal that is shot must be reported and as soon the quota is reached, the hunt is cancelled. But there are more rules. Every hunter, for example, must be in the possession of a diploma or licence, the maximum shooting distance is 100 metres and the chance that the animal is killed immediately must be realistic. Hunters are not allowed to wound an animal and let it walk away. If the hunter does not keep to the rules, his/her permit will be confiscated immediately. However, despite the strict rules and the considerate approach, the hunt is extremely traumatic for the moose, and after having survived the hunting season in their first year, they will be scared of people for the rest of their lives.

EVERYMAN'S RIGHT

It is a great Swedish good: everyman's right. Traditionally, hikers are allowed to walk almost everywhere and people are allowed to camp in the wild. However, everyman's right is not regulated by law, but a 'habit', without a legal basis. In practice, this makes its use more complicated than it might seem. For example, it does not give you the right to walk straight through someone's garden and the regional government can also determine some areas as not accessible. For example because of nature conservation or dangerous situations (swamp).

Another complicating factor is that a relatively large area (circa 33%) of Swedish soil is owned by companies or private persons that use the areas for commercial reasons such as forestry; and of course they are not always pleased about the frequent use made of their grounds, without getting any profit out of it. In order to prevent any problems we have chosen to include and describe only pre-existing routes in this guide and in this way you can be sure that permission is given for a

walking route. Moreover, these routes are almost all (concisely) marked.
However, because you will be walking on privately owned grounds, we would like to give you several useful and hopefully obvious tips:
- Leave animals and plants alone. Do not pick any flowers or berries.
- Do not cause any damage to the forests and follow the paths as much as possible.
- Do not drop any litter.
- Do not make a (camp) fire outside the indicated areas (near shelters).
- Do not get in the way of foresters and other people at work.
  Always ask permission to pass if you want to cross the ground they are working on.
- You are a guest, so therefore behave as one.

PRACTICAL
Walking in Värmland can be pretty challenging and because of the hilly terrain and often difficult subsoil you probably will not walk much more than 2.5 to 3 km per hour. For each walk we have indicated what the distance is, and how long it took us, without taking into account any breaks; so make sure you select routes and distances and that match your 'walking experience'.
All walks are tours. In three cases (walks 6, 14 and 19) the routes can be shortened and the itinerary indicates how you can select the shorter option. Värmland is vast and thinly populated and most villages can be reached by bus, but there is not a regular bus service. Points of departure for our walks are mostly far from any bus routes or stops and in order to reach these points you will need a (rental)car.

WHAT DO YOU TAKE WITH YOU?
First of all this guide; but there are a couple of matters you should also keep in mind when you go out on a walking tour. The weather in Sweden can vary greatly; sometimes rainy and cold, but sometimes it is incredibly hot. In the latter case you should take into account that in the spring and summer the sun shines considerably longer, and from a different angle, than elsewhere in Western Europe. At 18.00 p.m. it still can be pretty hot here, so take plenty of water

with you (at least 0.75 litres per person), suntan lotion and a cap or a hat. Furthermore, as there are not many places where you can get something to eat you should also take sufficient food with you. Good walking shoes are important, preferably waterproof, because almost all routes will take you through swampy, peat-like areas. On rainy days, or when the weather is inconsistent, it is also wise to take a rain jacket. Also convenient are long (convertible) trousers, as you will often walk through bushes or across over-grown paths. Finally: walking in Värmland is an isolated and quiet activity and if some-thing happens to you underway, for example if you were to break a leg, it could literally take days before someone would find you. The network of Swedish mobile operators has a good overall coverage, so do not leave your mobile phone at home! As elsewhere in Europe, the Swedish emergency phone number is 112.

GPS AND MAPS

The Lantmäteriet, the Swedish topographical service, has done an excellent job of mapping the country and many detailed maps are available. A disadvantage is the fact that you have to buy quite a lot of different maps in order to cover the entire province and that is rather expensive. The maps in this book, in combina-tion with the itinerary, provide sufficient information to follow the routes without any other maps. For GPS users we have in-cluded a limited number of points as support per walk; but the use of GPS is not necessary for these walks!

FOR WHO?

These walks are suited for people who are reasonably fit. For each walk we have indi-cated the level of difficulty: 1 = easy, 2 = average, 3 = difficult. These indications are based on matters such as length of the route, the degree of ascent and descent and the 'discomfort' (for example bad subsoil) with which you are confronted. The routes almost always consist of unpaved paths, but sometimes you will be able to walk along asphalt roads. However, the routes are not suitable for people who have walking problems or for prams.

WALKING FURTHER

As stated before, walking in Sweden is not a problem; but rather the fact that there is a lack of clearly described routes. Many of the routes that have been plotted are long distance paths of which we mention a couple below. Almost all paths are marked with orange paint.

Finnskogleden
240 km long route along the Swedish-Norwegian border.
Nord-Värmlandsleden
54 km route through the north of the province.
Pilgrimsleden
Long route, from Karlstad (Sweden) to Trondheim (Norway), goes through Värmland and follows for the most part the run of Klarälven river.
Glaskogen Naturreservat
This area has more than 300 km of marked walking paths. Mostly from A to Z, but tours are also possible. Walks 7 and 9 go through this area. A general map can be obtained from the information centre in Lenungshammar.

GPS COORDINATES WALK 1 - HILLS AROUND LAKE ÄNGEN

1. Parking place car	N 59 52.514 • E 12 48.150	5. Immigrant houses	N 59 51.160 • E 12 48.857
2. Brook	N 59 52.205 • E 12 49.084	6. Branching with signposts	N 59 52.193 • E 12 46.283
3. Stone bridge	N 59 51.756 • E 12 50.136	7. Grass path	N 59 53.153 • E 12 46.287
4. Gravel road	N 59 51.279 • E 12 50.868		

	DISTANCE:	16.3 km
1	TYPE:	tour
	TIME:	ca 5.5 hours
	DIFFICULTY:	3 (distance, climbing/descending)

ÄNGEN

Hills around Lake Ängen

GETTING THERE

Take off the 45 (the main road through Värmland) the exit Gräsmark/Ski Sunne, coming from Karlstad direction Torsby. After 12.4 km take the exit left to Ängen, a gravel road. After 9.5 km you will pass the sign 'Ängen' and 200 metres further on you take a right turn. Follow the signs 'Rokkmakkstugan'. Go left after 1.4 km, and again left after 300 metres. After 500 metres you will see a sign that points to the right to the Rokkmakkstugan. Park your car to the right, alongside the road.

WHY?

A beautiful and brisk walk, in the middle of nature. This well-marked route takes you across narrow paths, straight through the forests, almost literally into the footsteps of the moose that live here. Every now and then you will cross an unpaved road, but as far as the human touch is concerned, that is about it. The route takes you along the remains of the cottages of Finnish immigrants who settled here between 1500 and 1600. Another highlight is the Nord Ängens Gruva, an old copper mine. Because of the climbing and descending you will not go any faster than about 2.5 km per hour. If you regularly take a break, this tour takes up most of the day. It can be pretty swampy here in the spring, so make sure you are wearing good waterproof shoes.

THE WALK

From the place where you have parked your car **(GPS1)** you turn right and take the road up to Rokkmakkstugan. After 50 metres you will see an information sign on your right. Just before that you turn right, on to the path 'Ängenleden' which is marked with orange paint. From here you keep following the marking: orange paint on posts and tree trunks. Walk down the forest path. A little further on you will cross a semi-paved road. Continue on the path past the electricity pylons. After 25 metres you cross a duckboard and immediately turn right. Further on, you go left up the slope via a narrow path. Keep your eyes on the orange marking. The path descends. You will come to a broader path and turn left here. You will now come to a gravel road which you must cross diagonally to the right. Follow the narrow, winding forest path that goes up and down. Keep to the right. On a hill top, where the marking is not very clear, you go diagonally to the right, straight between two pine trees. A little further on you will again see the orange marking. The path descends and comes to a broader path and a brook **(GPS2)**. On the right is the Ängsjön. You continue straight on, across the brook and up again, a long and sometimes steep climb. Sometimes you will be able to see the lake. You will reach a viewpoint with a picnic bench. Continue on the path that descends here. After some time you can see a couple of houses to your left. Keep right here. After 200 metres you will come to a gravel road. Cross this and follow, through the bushes, the orange marking. Further on, the path becomes clearer. Pass a brook via a little stone bridge **(GPS3)**. Take a right turn immediately after that, on to a narrow duckboard. At the end of the duckboard you turn left, in the direction of 'Fångstgropar'. The path winds up. There is a crossing with a broader path and further on, a cart track. Turn left here and right again after 10 metres. Further on, you will walk through a cut down stretch of forest. Continue through the field following the orange marking which is still visible on the tree stumps. You will reach a gravel road **(GPS4)**, which you cross diagonally and to the right, into the direction of the waterfall. Follow the marking towards the waterfall and cross this via the little bridge. Go right immediately after that. The path starts going up. After about one kilometre you will reach a gravel road. Here, you take a right turn and a left turn after 20 metres, straight into the forest. Further on, you see left, in the distance, a wooden house. Follow the marking which takes you straight into the forest. Via a ditch you will come to a gravel road. Here you take a left turn. Past the drive to the house you go left into the forest, past a picnic table. When you come to an open area, you more or less go straight on, underneath the house. Pay attention to the marking leading you down the slope. You reach a gravel path. Turn left here and right again after 30 metres, up the slope. The path is hardly visible here; follow the orange marking on the tree stumps going up. At the top you go straight on and then down the hill again. The narrow path twists through the forest, between the ruins of two Finnish immigrant houses **(GPS5)**. You reach an

open space where you turn right. At a crossing near a wooden shed you turn left. A little further on you will reach a branching with signposts. Turn right here: Ängenleden. Further on, you cross a narrow duckboard. After some time you will see the lake through the trees. A little further on you can see a shelter on the right. You will reach a broader grassy path. Here you will go left and up and a little further on right again into the forest. The path twists up. Further on, you will see signposts again. Go straight on: Ängenleden. Before reaching a picnic bench, the path turns to the right. It twists and reaches an open field with small sheds. Cross the field and walk towards a little wall. Here you enter the forest again. The path meanders down and comes to a branching with signposts **(GPS6)**. Turn left here: Ängenleden. Further on, you cross a duckboard. After that the path twists further and after about 20 minutes you will, after a short climb, reach a picnic bench. The path goes left here. Go onto the hill and after that straight down again. You will reach a path. Turn right here. Further on, you will cross a narrow duckboard. Continue the narrow path straight ahead that runs almost straight through the deforested area. You will now reach what looks like a parking place. Cross this towards the gravel road. Here you turn right and after 100 metres left again into the forest. Keep

an eye on the orange marking. The path is mostly overgrown here but the marking clear enough to keep you going. You will reach a branching with a broader grass path **(GPS7)**. Here you turn right. Cross a gravel road and go straight into the forest. Ignore paths on either side and follow the marking. Further on the path will become broader. Keep to your right, the path descends here. You will reach a gravel road. Take a left turn here and immediately after that a right turn at the signpost: Ängenleden. A little further on there is a shelter on the right. Just behind that you will cross the grounds of an old mine. Keep the water-filled craters to your right and cross the grounds. On the other side, the orange marking will lead you into the forest again via a narrow path. Further on you will reach a gravel road, where you turn left. Walk between the houses of a hamlet. Although it is difficult to see the marking, keep following the road. After almost one kilometre you will see to your right a signpost that sends you to the right to the Rokkmakkstugan. Go into the forest and go left after 300 metres. You will come to the back of the Rokkmakkstugan. Walk straight past it and follow the gravel path down. You will now come to the gravel road where your car is parked on the left **(GPS1)**.

GPS COORDINATES WALK 2 - TO LAKE ABBORTTJÄRNET

1. Parking place car	N 60°00.937 • E 12°42.260	4. Gravel road	N 60°01.296 • E 12°40.804
2. Gravel road	N 60°01.344 • E 12°42.593	5. Signpost 'Kvarna'	N 60°00.830 • E 12°40.341
3. Path right downwards	N 60°01.411 • E 12°41.575	6. Branching	N 60°00.475 • E 12°41.776

DISTANCE:	8.3 km
TYPE:	tour
TIME:	ca 2.5 hours
DIFFICULTY:	1

TIMBONÄS

To Lake Abborttjärnet

GETTING THERE

From the 45 (the main road through Värmland) take the exit Gräsmark. Continue until in Gräsmark and follow the signs Torsby from there. At the exit Torsby you head into the direction of Mitandersfors. After 10.9 km you will pass the sign Timbonäs. After 400 metres you turn right at the sign Kammesmakk, on to a gravel road. After 700 metres, near a couple of letterboxes, take the narrow road to the left. After 400 metres, park your car right alongside the road, at the beginning of the grass path and near an information sign.

21

WHY?

This part of Värmland is a maze of short, badly kept footpaths. For this walk we have connected several of them, thus forming a tour. All paths are moderately kept and marked (spring 2008). This is sometimes inconvenient, but it also gives you the feeling that you are the only one making use of them, together with the many moose that live here. Lake Abborttjärnet is a beautiful oasis which you can enjoy in silence. For a large part, the walk crosses the grounds owned by the people that live in the houses you will see. Appreciate their hospitality and respect their privacy.

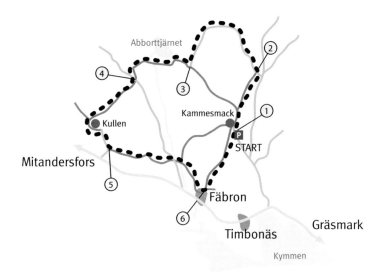

THE WALK

Walk from the car **(GPS1)** straight onto the grass path, past an information sign. Keep the shed to your left. The path is marked with orange stripes. After 300 metres you will cross a gravel path and further on, near a signpost 'Honkamack 1800 m', you must turn right. Walk into the pine forest. Further on, ignore a path to the left. Follow the descending path that goes straight ahead. Ignore side-paths and follow the orange marking. You will come to a gravel road **(GPS2)**. Turn left here. Follow this road, 1.8 km long, until the end. About 100 metres before you reach the end, take the descending path on your right **(GPS3)**. This one too, is marked with orange paint. The path is overgrown, but further on you will again be able to see the marking. Cross a brook via a small jetty. In front of you is Lake Abborrtjärnet. Keep right. The path reaches a narrow bridge across the brook. Cross the bridge and keep following the marking until you reach a crossing with a broader grass path. Here you turn left. You then reach a broad gravel road. Turn left here and after 30 metres take a sharp turn to the right on to a gravel road **(GPS4)** (orange marking). This road goes up with a curve. Near a couple of houses you keep to your left and follow the marking into the forest, on to a broad grassy path. Ignore side-paths and keep following the marking. The path becomes very narrow and is overgrown. You will reach and open area near a shed. Keep this to your right and walk straight on, underneath the electricity cables. Keep the electricity pylons to your left and continue straight ahead. On top of the slope you can see signposts on your right. Take a left turn here and walk right past the electricity pylon. You now walk around the Kullen house. Follow the (limited) orange marking here. Near the shed the path turns right and a little further on at a new signpost it goes to the left. You will now come to a gravel road, where you turn right. After about 200 metres you turn left, on to an over-grown grassy path, near the signpost 'Kvarna' **(GPS5)**. The path goes into the forest; as soon as you have reached the edge of the forest you turn right. When you come to the new plantings you go straight ahead and further on, at a signpost, left. The path turns right, keep following the orange marking. The path descends and at the bottom you keep right. You will come a to broad gravel road. Here you turn right and near the house and the signpost you turn left. Cross the river via the bridge. Once on the other side, turn right, in the direction of Fäbron. After 50 metres you go straight ahead and up via a narrow path. A little further on you have a good view of the river. The path turns left near a wooden shed and reaches a couple of houses. Turn left here, along the edge of the forest and keep the houses to your right. Near the last house, the path branches off **(GPS6)**. Take a sharp left turn again, into the forest. Follow the orange marking. The path is sometimes barely visible here. Where the old forest changes into young plantings you go right and up. Continue straight ahead and cross a broader path with electricity pylons. The path is very narrow and sometimes difficult to find. Pay close attention to the orange marking which is hardly present here. Further on, the path descends and you will cross a stream. Continue the narrow path until you reach the edge of the forest and a pasture. Here you go diagonally to the right and up. Walk on, and continue until you reach the gravel road. Your car is parked on the right **(GPS1)**.

GPS COORDINATES WALK 3 - SEVEN 'FINNISH VILLAGES' AT THE SWEDISH-NORWEGIAN BORDER			
1. Information sign	N 60°08.519 • E 12°33.327	4. Lebiko	N 60°09.153 • E 12°30.752
2. Sign '7-torps'	N 60°08.439 • E 12°32.466	5. Kissalamp	N 60°09.456 • E 12°31.931
3. Swedish-Norwegian border	N 60°08.715 • E 12°31.236		

LEKVATTNET

Seven 'Finnish villages' at the Swedish-Norwegian border

GETTING THERE

From the 45 (the main road through Värmland) take the exit Lekvattnet near Torsby. Drive on via the 239 until you reach Lekvattnet. In the village you turn left at the exit Simonstorp/Ritamäki. Across the lake you turn right, the road becomes semi-paved here. After 7.4 km you turn right at the sign Ritamäki. After 2.7 km you will see information signs, near the edge of Lake Lomsen. You can park you car here.

25

WHY?

A relatively short walk during which you will become acquainted with the specific Finnskogen culture. This walk partly follows the Finnskogsleden, the 240 km long distance path through the Swedish-Norwegian border region. In the 17th century, when Sweden and Finland were still one country, Finnish nomads settled in this uninhabited region. The seven 'villages' are remains of small settlements, often not more than one house, where 10 to 15 people lived. During this walk you will cross the Swedish-Norwegian border for a moment. Nature in this area is rougher and more mountainous than in the green heart of Värmland.

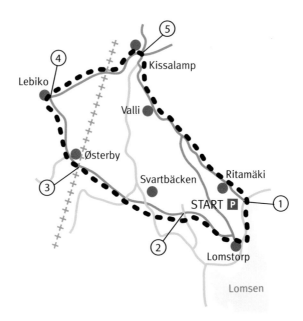

THE WALK

With your face towards the information signs **(GPS1)** turn left. From here, follow the
signs '7-torpsleden'. You will walk on a gravel road along the water. Soon you will see
Lomstorp, left at the waterside. Here, you take a sharp right turn near the sign '7-torps',
and go up via a narrow grassy path. At a crossroad near some wooden sheds you go
diagonally to the left, near the sign '7-torps'. You follow a narrow path, past a wooden
shed. Further on the path becomes broader and you will pass a picnic bench. Keep following the path until you reach, via a wooden jetty, a broad semi-paved road. Cross this
road and continue the path at the sign '7-torp' **(GPS2)**. Further on, you go into the forest
and cross a brook via a little bridge. You will then come to Svartbäcken, near a couple
of houses. Continue the path along the edge of the pine forest. Past the last building
the path descends to the left. You will reach a gravel road. Turn left here. At a T-junction
you take a left turn and 50 metres further on you turn right, at the '7-torps' sign, on to
a grass path. Further on, you will cross a gravel road and go straight ahead and up via
a grassy path. A little further on, you must cross a ditch by means of a jetty. Continue
on the path. A bit further on you will pass the Swedish-Norwegian border **(GPS3)**. Keep
following the descending path, by means of several jetties, until you reach a house
and sheds: Østerby. Head straight on, past the sign and follow the blue marking from
here. Follow this path for quite some time until you reach the wooden houses of Lebiko

(GPS4). Before you reach the big wooden house you turn right, in the direction of Kissalamp. Keep following the blue-orange marking. The path twists through the forest and you will regularly walk across jetties and duckboards. You will again cross the Norwegian-Swedish border. Continue following the path until you reach the house and sign 'Kissalamp' **(GPS5)**. Take a right turn here, in the direction of Valli. After 150 metres you turn left at a junction. After 500 metres you reach the overgrown remains of Valli. Walk to the right, to the back of 'the house'. After that, continue the path and go on until you reach a wooden fence. Go through the fence and follow the path that turns left and right through nature reserve Ritamäki. Follow the blue-orange marking. You will reach the wooden houses and sheds. The path continues, along the fence and the shed, until the end of the field. Here you go through the fence and continue the descending path. Further on you will pass a small stream via flagstones. Continue following the descending path until you reach the information signs and parking place where your car is parked **(GPS1)**.

GPS COORDINATES WALK 4 - THE RACKSTAD MOUNTAINS AND LAKE AGVATTNET

1. Parking place car	N 59°41.567 • E 12°40.797	5. Gravel road	N 59°42.442 • E 12°43.215
2. Viewpoint	N 59°41.861 • E 12°40.996	6. Broad path	N 59°40.740 • E 12°43.121
3. Göpommen	N 59°42.217 • E 12°41.678	7. Crossing	N 59°41.249 • E 12°41.635
4. Broad path to right	N 59°42.649 • E 12°41.637		

ARVIKA

The Rackstad Mountains and Lake Agvattnet

GETTING THERE

From Arvika, take the road to Karlstad on the roundabout at the McDonalds. A little further on, you take the exit left to Gunnarskog and the airport. After 2.6 km you turn right at the exit Rackstad. Follow the road for 3.3 km and turn right at the sign Jössestugan. Go to the parking place and park your car.

WHY?

A beautiful mountainous walk during which you will bridge a difference in height of about 150 metres. The slopes are covered with currant bushes, but in the spring you can also see lots of lilies-of-the-valley. From various points you can get a beautiful view of Lake Racken and the surrounding area. When the weather is clear you can see for miles. Also special is Svartmossen, a peat moor, with its very own vegetation. In the spring lots of common cotton grass grows here. There are not many moose, but wolves can be found here. However, because these animals are so shy you can only see them running away in the distance, if you are lucky. You will be able to see their footprints in the mud.

THE WALK

From the parking place **(GPS1),** you take the gravel path past the barrier. After 100 metres you go left at the Jössestugan and walk between the house and the shed. When you come to the tree with the signs you go straight ahead in the direction of 'Racken-utsikten'. On your right is a steep rock mass. Keep to your right and follow the orange marking. When you have reached the top you go left at the crossing. On the T-crossing you go left again. The path goes up, sometimes quite steep. Via the narrow path you will reach the viewpoint **(GPS2)** over Lake Racken. With your back towards the lake you walk straight on, up the orange-marked path. This path meanders for almost 1.2 km through the forest until Göpommen **(GPS3)**. There you go diagonally to the left at the tree with the little sign. Follow the orange marking. The path descends and further on you will walk through an area with cut down trees. Keep following the path and the marking. You will reach a broader path and take a right turning. Keep following this path for about 800 metres. The orange marking will direct you to the right, on to a broad path **(GPS4)**. Walk down this path straight to Lake Agvattnet. Here you turn left and fol-low the path for more than 1 km along the banks of the lake (orange marking). You will pass a wooden cabin twice. Further on, the path bends away from the lake and you will reach a gravel road **(GPS5)**. Turn right and ignore a path to the right. A little further on you take a narrow descending path (orange marking) to the right. After 25 metres you will cross a path and here you go straight on, onto the ascending path. You will now reach a terrain where the trees have been cut down. Keep following the orange marking here. Further on the path becomes broader and you will shortly walk through the peat via a duckboard. The path leads into the forest again. You will come to a gravel road. Here you turn left. At the end of the gravel road you take a left turning. Ignore the first path on the right (after 15 metres) with orange marking and keep following the gravel road. From here you start following the dark green marking. After about 100 metres you turn diagonally to the right, on to a narrow path between young trees. The path is overgrown, but after about 60 metres you will see on your left a tree stump with a green dot. Keep following this path, that twists through the bushes. It is sometimes difficult to see the green marking and the path is very narrow and overgrown. Via some tree trunks you will pass a ditch twice. Further on, the path becomes more visible and twists through the forest. Continue following the path until you reach viewpoint 'Djupdalshöjden'. Continue the path across the mountain ridge. Further on, the path starts descending. After some time you will see a broad path to the left **(GPS6)**. Here, you continue straight on across the narrow path. This is the most southern point of the walk. Continue following the green marked path. The path becomes broader and you will reach a gravel road. Turn left and after 20 metres right again, on to a narrow forest path. After 100 metres you will reach a crossing **(GPS7)**. From here you will also see the orange marking again. Turn left and further on, on a Y-crossing, turn right on to a narrow path. The path twists through the forest and descends. Via a long duckboard track you will pass a brook. On the next crossing you turn left, and down. You will reach the Jössestugan. Walk straight on to the parking place where your car is parked **(GPS1)**.

GPS COORDINATES WALK 5 - AROUND LAKE SÖDRA HYN AND ALONG KLARÄLVEN RIVER

1. Parking place	N 59°27.906 • E 13°22.832	4. Narrow forest path	N 59°29.482 • E 13°25.296
2. Road bends to left	N 59°28.104 • E 13°22.496	5. Service road	N 59°28.629 • E 13°24.655
3. Semi-paved road	N 59°30.180 • E 13°23.171		

KIL

Around Lake Södra Hyn and along Klarälven River

GETTING THERE

Coming from Arvika in the direction of Karlstad on the E61, you take the exit Hynboholm/Flyplats. Turn left, underneath the road; go straight ahead and further on underneath the railway track. Go left to Hynboholm. Turn right at the sign Södra Hyns Strandängar/Grava Hembygdsgard. You will arrive at a parking area and some information signs. Park your car here.

WHY?

A relatively easy walk through the southern part of Värmland which can be combined with a visit to Karlstad, the capital of the province. It is one of the few walks going through an agricultural area. You will walk partly through fields and pastures and have excellent view of the green surroundings. Near Acksjön you will shortly walk across the track of the first Swedish railway line, which dates back to 1849. After that you will, for some time, follow the run of the Klarälven, a long river that cuts through Värmland from north to south. Along the banks of the river you will be able to see the tracks of the beavers that live here. In spring, you can see all kinds of wildflowers and roadside flowers, such as lupins and wild geraniums. Because part of the walk goes through high grass (with nettles!), it is wise to wear trousers.

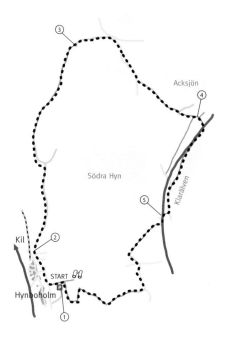

Acksjön

Södra Hyn

Klarälven

Kil

START

Hynboholm

THE WALK

Facing the information sign **(GPS1)** you turn left. Turn left again at the orange marking. Near the last shed of the Hembygdsgård you go right, towards the viewpoint. Continue the walk by turning left here. Follow the narrow path between the trees. At the asphalt road you turn right. When the road bends to the left **(GPS2)**, you turn right and straight after that left again, on to a no-through asphalt road along the railway track. Further on, the asphalt road becomes a gravel road. You will pass some houses and keep following the road with orange marking. The main road turns to the left. Ignore a side-road to the right. Keep following the path. A little further on you will walk between some sheds and take a left turn. You now walk on a broad grass path going into the forest. Further on, the path becomes quite narrow. Follow this path for a few kilometres until you reach a semi-paved road near some houses **(GPS3)**. You now walk on a road past some (holi-day) cottages. Ignore side-roads and continue following the orange marking. In a curve to the right you take a narrow path to the left, which leads to an asphalt road. You walk alongside the road and turn right at the first asphalt road that goes to the right. Follow this road and ignore side-roads. After some time, just behind a house on the left, the marking sends you left, on to a semi-paved path. Walk straight on and follow the path with the orange marking. The path bends to the right and a little further on you can see Lake Acksjön. At a crossing you take the narrow path with orange marking to the right. Ignore side-roads and walk straight on until the orange marking sends you to the right, on to a narrow forest path **(GPS4)**. This path continues until just before the asphalt road. Here, you turn right and 100 metres further on you take a left turn, towards the asphalt road. Cross this and turn right immediately after that. Follow the marking that leads you to a narrow path along Klarälven River. Follow this path for some time. Just after passing a picnic bench you take a path to the right. You will now come to an asphalt road which runs parallel with the main road. Turn left here. After more than 500 metres you turn right via an orange marked gravel road, towards the main through road. Cross this and turn left on the service road **(GPS5)**.

Where the asphalt road curves to the right, you go straight on towards a field. Turn right just before the field and follow a narrow path along the edge. Where this path bends to the right, you continue for 50 metres along the field and follow the orange marking to the right. The path descends and then goes up again. Continue on the path and keep to your left when you reach a crossing. The path comes to a broader path. Here you go straight on. Ignore side-roads and continue following the orange marking. You will pass a barrier. Go straight on until you reach the asphalt road where you turn right. You will pass houses and farms. Behind a couple of sheds on your left, the orange marking takes you to the right, towards a path along a brook. Further on, you go left, on to a little embankment, alongside the brook. Keep following the marking and walk to the right, around a shed, and continue the path over the embankment. At the end of this path you take a sharp right turn, along the edge of the field. At the end, you turn left across the water via a wooden bridge and immediately after that you turn to the right. Further on, you take a left turn again and at the end you cross the water via another wooden bridge. Turn right a little further on, on to a narrow path and towards the parking area **(GPS1)**.

GPS COORDINATES WALK 6 - THROUGH THE PEAT AND PAST OLD MINES

1. Parking place 1	N 59°56.592 • E 12°41.347	4. Five way junction	N 59°55.296 • E 12°44.493
2. Gravel road	N 59°56.097 • E 12°42.037	5. Broad sandy road	N 59°54.510 • E 12°43.625
3. Parking place 2	N 59°55.749 • E 12°43.403	6. Remains stone cottage	N 59°55.057 • E 12°42.799

6

WALK

DISTANCE: 8.2 or 14.0 km
TYPE: tour
TIME: ca 3.5 or 5 hours
DIFFICULTY: 2 or 3 (climbing/descending, subsoil, distance)

GRÄSMARK

Through the peat and past old mines

GETTING THERE

From the 45 (main road through Värmland), coming from Karlstad in the direction of Torsby, take the exit Gräsmark/Ski Sunne. Just before Gräsmark take the exit to Arvika. After some time you will a sign to your right: 'L:a Tinhöjden'. Turn left after 1.2 km, on to a gravel road. Park your car here. For a shorter variant you drive on to the gravel road and continue for 2.7 km until you reach a parking area on the right side of the road. Specifications of the shorter route will be given after the extra spacing in the text.

37

WHY?

During this walk you will see the traces that were left behind in the landscape by 400 years of mining history. As early as 1550, people were already searching for copper and iron in this area. The last mine was closed down in 1899. Since then, the mining shafts have become overgrown and/or filled with water, and have thus become part of the natural landscape again. If you choose the longer variant of the route, you will first walk through a peat area for three kilometres. This is swampy subsoil with its own specific vegetation, including orchids in early summer. The route will take you partly through heavily overgrown paths. Long trousers are a necessity here, as are waterproof shoes.

THE WALK

Go diagonally to the left at the signpost 'Tiskaretjärn 7 km', onto the path with orange marking. Follow this marking during the entire route. The path goes right and passes a brook. Further on you will go through swampy high moorland. On a crossing with a semi-paved path you go right. On a gravel road you turn left and after 15 metres you go right, into the forest. Follow the orange marking. You will pass a stream and further on you will come through a forest clearing. The path is hardly visible here, so pay close attention to the marking. The path twists across the terrain, shortly goes into the forest and then reaches open grounds again. Keep left. You will come to a gravel road **(GPS2)**. Turn right and go left after 75 metres, on to a narrow path with orange marking. Keep following this path straight on and ignore all side-roads. You will pass a sign '42'. There are benches to the right. Go straight on here and follow the orange marking. On a broader grass path you take a right turn and after 30 metres a left turn, on to a narrow path. Turn right on a broad overgrown path. Keep left at the crossing. You will reach another crossing with signs. Here you turn left in the direction of 'Tiskaretjärn 4 km'. You will now come to an open area with gravel. This is the parking place **(GPS3)** where the short route begins.

Cross the road and walk into the forest near the orange marking. After about 100 metres you will reach the Kattgruvan. Continue along the path and cross the gravel road once

more. Go straight on, on to a broad path. Keep left at the Y-junction (orange marking), an overgrown grassy path. Further on, near the Källare Gruvan facility, you
go left. Walk between the mining pit and the picnic bench and follow the orange
marking into the forest. You cross a sand road and continue straight on, through the
trees and bushes. The path goes left into the forest again. Near a little bench you go
straight on. The path descends. Further on, the path bends to the right and twists
through the forest. Go down to the banks of Lake Mången. On your left you will see
a ruin and on your right a picnic bench. Go straight on and keep following the orange
marking. The path continues until you reach a five way junction **(GPS4)**. Take the first
ascending path to the right, in the direction of 'Gruvrundan'. After a brisk climb, go
left on to a narrow path (orange marking). The ascending path twists through the
forest. You will pass a few small quarries and cross a broad path. After some time,
you will reach the sign '146', the Asphöjdsgruvan. Continue on the twisting, ascending and descending path through the forest. After a steep descent, on an overgrown
path, you will reach a broad gravel road near Storgruvan. Cross the road and go
straight on between the fence and the picnic bench. Go past the mine and turn right
into the forest. Continue following the marking. You will reach open ground with
remains of a mine. On the right you can see Lake Abbortjärn. After a steep descend
you will come to a broad sandy road **(GPS5)**. Go right here, and after 20 metres, right
again. The path runs alongside the slope and winds through the forest a little further
on. Keep following the orange marking until you reach a broad gravel road. Go left
and immediately to the right again, into the forest. Keep left here. Follow the path.
Cross another path and go straight on. Turn right on a broader grass path and, after
75 metres, turn to the left. Follow the forest path for quite some time. You will pass
another quarry and the remains of a stone cottage **(GPS6)**. A bit further on you turn
left at a crossing, on to a broad grass path. Keep following this path until you reach
a crossing of paths with road signs. Here you go right (again). After about 100 metres
you will reach the parking area **(GPS3)**. This is the end of the short route. For the
longer route, go left on the gravel road and follow this for 2.7 km. Ignore side-roads
and walk to your car **(GPS1)**.

GPS COORDINATES WALK 7 · THE SOUTHEAST OF GLASKOGENS NATURRESERVAT

1. Parking area	N 59°26.206 • E 12°33.812	4. Tithöjden	N 59°24.737 • E 12°33.548
2. Shelter	N 59°25.767 • E 12°34.133	5. Crossing with broader path	N 59°25.175 • E 12°32.660
3. Holtjärnskojan	N 59°24.950 • E 12°34.183		

7 WALK

DISTANCE: 7.5 km
TYPE: tour
TIME: ca 3.5 hours
DIFFICULTY: 2 (climbing/descending)

GÄNGENE
The southeast of Glaskogens Naturreservat

GETTING THERE

From the information centre in Lenungshammar you continue along the road in the direction of Sölje. After 8.5 km you take the exit to Sölje. After 7.4 km you go left and then after 3.9 km you take a sharp right turning at the sign Gängene. After 200 metres you turn left. After 300 metres, you will see a cabin on your left and a fire place. Left of the road is an open area. You can park your car here.

WHY?

Glaskogens Naturreservat is the largest continuous protected nature reserve of Värmland. The area is situated southwest of Arvika and consists for a large part of bigger and smaller lakes. The area is ideal for canoe tours and walking tours. The area has a great many marked routes, including longer walks (of several days). We have described two routes for this area: this short route and a longer one (walk 9). It is compulsory to buy a day-ticket from the information centre in Lenungshammar or from the tourist information office in Arvika (SEK 30 = € 3.50 in 2010). Both also sell a general map with several marked walks.

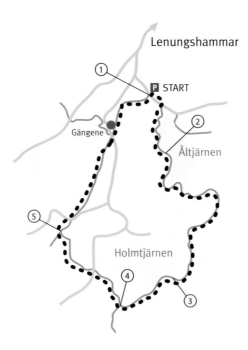

Lenungshammar

①

P START

②

Gängene

Åltjärnen

⑤

Holmtjärnen

④

③

THE WALK

From the parking area **(GPS1)** you continue on the gravel road. After 250 metres, at the blue signposts, you turn right, in the direction of 'Sulerud 12'. Follow the orange marking from here. The path twists through the forest. On the left you can see Lake Åltjärnen. Further on you will walk closely along the water and then reach a shelter **(GPS2)**. Walk around the shelter and continue the path. For a while, you will follow the edge of the lake. Further on, you will pass some big rocks and a waterfall. Cross a brook via a wooden bridge and keep left, in the direction of the lake. Continue along the path beside the banks of the lake. Further on, the path goes up, away from the lake. You now walk across the ridge of the hill. Down to the right you can see a little lake. Further on, there is a steep descent, along a wooden banister. You will cross a swampy area via wooden duckboards twice. Further on, the path goes up again; twisting through the forest until it reaches a lake. Keep following the orange marking. The path turns away from the lake and goes up again. Further on, you will again reach the banks of the lake. Keep following the path and the marking. You will pass an information sign about the Holtjärnskojan **(GPS3)**, a former cabin where forest workers used to live. Further on, the path descends again and reaches a small natural dam between two lakes. Here, you turn left and keep the lakes on your right. (Attention: the orange marking goes in two directions here). Follow the banks of the lake. Further on, the path goes up and across a waterfall. Walk through the forest and follow the orange marking. After some climbing, you will reach a crossing of paths: Tithöjden **(GPS4)**. Here you turn right, in the direction of 'Gängene 3'. The path descends. Cross a brook via duckboards. Keep following the path until you reach a gravel road. Cross this and follow the path up the hill. Keep following this path until you reach a lake. The orange marked path follows the banks of the lake here and goes into the bushes again further on. On a crossing with a broader path **(GPS5)** you turn right and go up. Cross a stream via a duckboard and continue along the path. You will now arrive at a crossing with a gravel road. Here you go right and up and then left after 100 metres, on to a forest path. Keep following this broad path straight ahead until you come to a house in an area with cleared trees. Here you go right and follow the orange marking across the terrain. You will reach a gravel road, near an information sign. Left from the sign, continue onto a narrow path, in the direction of Stömne. Follow the path and the marking. You will alternately walk through the forest and across an area of cleared trees. Via a duckboard you will pass a stream. Continue the ascending path. You will now reach a gravel road, right across from where you have parked your car **(GPS1)**.

43

GPS COORDINATES WALK 8 - THROUGH FORESTS AND ALONG THE HIGH MOORLAND

1. Crossing (car)	N 59°46.587 • E 12°49.401	5. Piled up rocks	N 59°48.810 • E 12°47.610
2. Crossing	N 59°46.371 • E 12°47.693	6. Broad grass path	N 59°48.559 • E 12°49.781
3. Broad grass path	N 59°47.682 • E 12°46.844	7. Semi-paved path	N 59°47.144 • E 12°49.552
4. Semi-paved road	N 59°48.568 • E 12°47.862		

MANGSKOG

Through forests and along the high moorland

GETTING THERE

From the 61, the road from Arvika to Karlstad, take the exit to Mangskog. On the crossing near the church in Mangskog you go straight on, in the direction of Västerrotna. After 2.5 km you will see the sign 'Tobyn'. After 200 metres you turn left at the sign 'Röstorp', on to a gravel road. Park your car here, by the side of the road, near the crossing.

WHY?

A beautiful and relatively easy walk across the pine-covered hills and through the peat areas in between. This part of Värmland is owned by one of the main forestry companies of Sweden, something that can be seen clearly in the landscape. In the spring, you can see between the pines, birches, moss and grass, the most diverse shades of green. You will mostly walk across broad, sloping paths without much climbing or descending. You are mostly accompanied by birds, little forest butterflies and, near brooks, dragonflies. When you pay attention to the footprints in the mud, you can see that there are moose here too.

Västerrotna

Nedre Flytjärnen

Gravtjärn

Fågeltjärnet

START **P**

Tobyn

Mangskog

THE WALK

From the crossing where your car is parked **(GPS1)** you continue along the gravel road and go straight on in the direction of Röstorp. To the left you see a small lake. Further on, at a Y-crossing, you take the descending left path. 450 metres further on, you turn left, on to a broad descending gravel path. Ignore a path to the right. At the end, on a crossing with a gravel road, you turn right, in the direction of a house. Walk past the house and take a narrow path, into the forest. Follow this path and keep left. The path descends towards a crossing **(GPS2)**, here you take a sharp right turn. The path is marked with orange paint. Follow this path for quite some time and ignore side-paths. At a crossing of four paths, go straight ahead and follow the marking. Further on, the path becomes overgrown and narrow. Keep following the path. Via a stone bridge you will pass a brook. On the right is the Fågeltjärnet (Bird Lake). Keep following the path until you reach a crossing with a broad and grassy path **(GPS3)**. Here you turn right. The path descends, ignore side-roads. When the path curves to the right, you take the broad path to the left (orange marking). Ignore the first path to the right and continue your walk going up. 30 metres further on is a Y-crossing. Take the path to the right, here. You will now walk on a narrow, winding path. Cross a brook and follow the marking. You will pass an old icehouse and then take a broader ascending path to the right. Almost immediately after that you turn left and after that right again in the direction of a shed. Walk past the shed and continue straight ahead. After about 20 metres, you turn left again on to a path with orange marking. Keep the house to your right and go left again on a broad path. A little further on you will pass a road sign. Go in the direction 'Porna 2 km'. On a broad path you turn left. Follow the orange marking. At a Y-crossing you take the left, lower, path. Further on this becomes a grass path. Ignore side-paths. Further on, you will walk through an area of cut down trees. Cross a stream via a jetty. The path curves to the right. You will walk past the remains of two stone cottages. You now reach a broad, semi-paved road **(GPS4)**. Here you turn right and 30 metres further on left again, on to a path with an orange marking. Further on, the path winds into the forest again. Near a row of piled up rocks **(GPS5)** you take a sharp right turn. This is where you leave the orange marking. Ignore any side-roads. Further on, you will occasionally be able to see orange marking on the trees again. You come to a broad semi-paved road. Turn left here. The road descends and at a T-crossing you must turn right. The road goes down here. Keep following this road for 1.8 km and ignore side-roads. Diagonally to your left you can see a gravel road coming on to this road. Continue straight on here. 100 metres further on you turn right, on to a broad grass path **(GPS6)**. This path is marked with orange paint again. Keep following this path until you reach a broad sand road. Cross this road, towards a cottage. Keep left and walk around the cottage, past the sheds. Continue the path straight ahead. There is no orange marking here, but a little further on it will reappear. You will pass a stream and further on an area of cleared trees. Keep following the broad path. Ignore a side-path to 'Tobyn Skola' and keep follow the path until you reach a crossing near a broad, semi-paved path **(GPS7)**. Here you go left. Keep following this road for about 1 km. You walk between the houses and after a while you will reach the crossing where your car is parked **(GPS1)**.

GPS COORDINATES WALK 9 - THE NORTHERN SIDE OF GLASKOGENS NATURRESERVAT

1. Building rifle club	N 59°32.261 • E 12°24.557	5. Banks Lake Stora	N 59°31.477 • E 12°27.838
2. Narrow path to left	N 59°32.685 • E 12°25.351	6. Shelter	N 59°31.419 • E 12°26.983
3. Töresbolsätern	N 59°32.619 • E 12°27.718	7. Viewpoint	N 59°31.713 • E 12°26.321
4. Asphalt road	N 59°32.186 • E 12°28.363	8. Broad grass path	N 59°31.820 • E 12°25.076

9

WALK

DISTANCE: 12.1 km
TYPE: tour
TIME: ca 4 hours
DIFFICULTY: 2 (distance, climbing)

GLAVA GLASBRUK

The northern side of Glaskogens Naturreservat

GETTING THERE

From the 172, the road from Arvika to Bengtsfors, take the exit to Glava. In Glava, ignore the exit to Lenungshammar and take the exit to Glava glasbruk a little further on, on the right. Drive through Glava glasbruk. At the first sign 'Halvarsnäs' the road becomes unpaved. After 3.9 km you will pass the second sign 'Halvarsnäs'. Turn right 100 metres further on. Park your car near the building of the rifle club.

49

WHY?

We have described two walks in the Glaskogens Naturreservat: a long and a short walk (walk 7). This walk takes you past two little lakes and to a viewpoint over Stora Gla, the biggest lake of Glaskogen. Halfway, you will see the buildings of the old glassworks. Until 1940, this was one of the biggest glassworks of Sweden, with approximately 500 employees. The building now houses a museum and gallery. It is compulsory to buy a day ticket for the Naturreservat at the Lenungshammar information centre or from the tourist office Arvika (SEK 30 = € 3.50 in 2010). Both also sell a general map with several marked walks.

THE WALK

Go from the building of the rifle club **(GPS1)** onto the gravel road. From here, the route is marked with orange paint. Walk past the small buildings and at the Y-crossing choose the path on the right. You will walk past a wooden shed. Where the path bends towards the house, you keep to the right, on a narrow grass path with orange marking. You go through a stretch of cut down forest and past a road sign. Follow the orange marking in the direction of 'Glava Glasbruk 5 km' to the right. You will alternately walk between trees and stretches of felled forest. Further on you will follow the orange marking, leave the broad path and go onto a narrow path to the left **(GPS2)**. You will reach a broader path. Keep left here, and further on, on a junction of paths, you go diagonally and straight on, onto the broad gravel road (orange marking). After about 200 metres, you get off the broad path and go diagonally to the left, onto a narrow path. Keep following this path. You will pass a brook twice and walk past the remains of a shed: Töresbolsätern **(GPS3)**. Follow the path. You pass a shelter and cross a duckboard three times. The path goes up. Further on, you can see Lake St. Skottjärnet. You will pass a brook and walk along the shores of the lake. Further on, the path bends away from the lake. Keep following the orange marking. Further on, the forest is partly felled. You will reach a broad gravel path. Here you should turn right. The path goes down and on the asphalt road **(GPS4)** you turn left. Follow the road for about 750 metres and go right at a road sign, onto a gravel road. On the corner is a canoe rental centre. Left of the road are the buildings of the old glassworks. Follow the orange marked gravel road alongside the houses. The road bends through the village. Ignore side-roads. At the end of the road you will reach the shores of Lake Stora Gla **(GPS5)**. Turn right onto a grass path and, near the blue road sign, immediately to the right again, in the direction of 'Vedviken'. Follow the path with the orange marking and ignore side-roads. The path goes up and winds through the forest. Further on, the path descends towards two small lakes: Sitjärnen. Follow the shores of the lakes until you reach a shelter **(GPS6)**. Continue the path along the shores, which partly crosses duckboards. Further on, the path bends away from the lake. After that you will cross a gravel road and continue along the narrow path with the orange marking. Via a duckboard you will cross a stream. The path goes up to the peak of the ridge and goes down immediately after that. Further on, the path goes up and down again until it comes to a broad gravel road. Cross this straight ahead and continue on the narrow path (orange marking). After a steep climb you will reach the hilltop and a viewpoint **(GPS7)**. Turn left at the picnic bench. Keep following the path. You will descend and reach a broad grass path, near the sign 'Halvardsnäs'. Here, you turn right and downwards. After 700 metres you will reach a gravel road. Go straight on here. Ignore side-roads. Further on, you will pass a house and a metal fence/barrier. Immediately after that you turn right, onto a broad grass path **(GPS8)**. Keep following the orange marking. Where the broad path bends to the right, you turn left onto a narrow path. This path descends towards a broad gravel road. Cross this and follow the narrow path into the forest. Continue walking until you reach a gravel road. Cross this, go straight on and walk towards your car **(GPS1)**.

GPS COORDINATES WALK 10 - AROUND THE STORKASBERGET

1. Look out tower	N 59°37.764 • E 12°38.558	4. Gravel road	N 59°36.164 • E 12°38.789
2. Wooden road sign	N 59°37.673 • E 12°39.492	5. Semi-paved road	N 59°36.977 • E 12°38.044
3. Broad sandy road	N 59°36.556 • E 12°39.728	6. Crossing near asphalt road	N 59°37.933 • E 12°37.149

ARVIKA
Around the Storkasberget

GETTING THERE

From Arvika, take the 175, in the direction of Säffle. Drive underneath the railway track, and after 300 metres turn left after the sign 'Utsiktstorn'. Turn right after 1.3 km, in the direction of 'Utsiktplats'. Ignore all side-roads and keep following the road upwards. Park your car in the parking area near the lookout tower.

53

WHY?

From the Storkasberget, you have an excellent view of Arvika and the lake. The mountainous area is not far from the town and is a recreational area for its inhabitants. It is also quiet enough to imagine yourself as being far away from civilization. Special plants, like Common Butterwort, a carnivorous plant, and vast forests make sure you feel like you are in the middle of nature. You can also find bigger inhabitants of the forest here such as moose. The walk is reasonably flat, with a brisk climb at the end and can be combined with a visit to the town or a sunny afternoon at the beach of nearby Ingenstrand.

THE WALK

From the parking area near the lookout tower **(GPS1)** you walk back a bit along the gravel road you came along in your car. After 200 metres, at the crossing, you take the gravel road to the right. After circa 900 metres and after a curve to the left, you go right at the wooden signpost **(GPS2)** with an orange marking, in the direction 'Örshulta'. Follow the narrow forest path with orange markings. You will see another signpost. Ignore side-paths. You will come to a gravel road. Head left here and after 10 metres you go to the right, in the direction 'Björnmyrastugan'. Follow the sparsely marked path with orange paint. At a crossing the markings go to the right; but you carry on in the direction Nordal, on an unmarked path. Further on, you will see the orange paint again. Ignore all side-paths and carry on up this path. You will reach a broad sandy road **(GPS3)** and you turn right here. You will walk along a metal fence until you reach a gravel road near a house. Go right here. Ignore a path to the right and follow the gravel road until you walk between some houses. Just after that you turn right, onto a gravel road **(GPS4)** and keep to the right here, in the direction of a house. Near the shed you go straight on, onto a broad path. Ignore all side-paths. Further on you will pass another house and sheds. Keep following the orange-marked path. Further on, ignore a side-path with orange markings to 'Björnmyren' and continue along the path. Turn left at a crossing with a semi-paved road **(GPS5)**. Lake Björntjärnet is on the right.

At a crossing with another gravel road you go straight on, in the direction of 'Käll-backen. The path becomes a forest path. You pass a brook. Ignore an exit to the right, to 'Storkasberget' and head straight on, in the direction of 'Ingenstrand'. Choose the orange-marked path to the right at a Y-crossing. Ignore side-paths and stay on the broad path, following the markings. Further on, you will see houses and you will pass a shed. Go straight on here on to the gravel road, in the direction of the asphalt road. Before the asphalt road you go right at a crossing **(GPS6)**. Further on, with view of the asphalt road, you go right again, onto a narrow forest path with orange markings. Ignore all side-paths. The path bends to the right. At a crossing of forest paths, you continue straight ahead, in the direction 'Storkasberget'. Follow the path with the orange markings and ignore all side-roads. Further ahead, a gradual climb begins. At a Y-crossing, choose the path to the left with orange markings. Ignore all side-paths. Turn right, in the direction 'Storkasberget' at the next Y-crossing. The climb gets steeper and eventually you will reach the peak of the mountain, at the foot of the lookout tower. Walk past the house, towards the parking area where your car is parked **(GPS1)**.

GPS COORDINATES WALK 11 · THE FINNTORPSLEDEN

1. Picnic table (car)	N 60°20.205 • E 12°40.682	4. Picnic table near Heikila	N 60°21.626 • E 12°38.194
2. Information sign	N 60°20.887 • E 12°38.936	5. Gravel road	N 60.22.085 • E 12°39.605
3. Gravel road	N 60°20.924 • E 12°38.390	6. Sign 'Kilbråten'	N 60°20.668 • E 12°40.227

11

WALK

DISTANCE:	10.7 km
TYPE:	tour
TIME:	ca 4 hours
DIFFICULTY:	2 (distance, badly kept paths)

ÖSTMARK

The Finntorpsleden

GETTING THERE

Östmark is situated northwest of Torsby. From Östmark, follow the road in the direction of Röjdåfors. 150 metres beyond the exit to Backsjön you can see a gravel road and picnic table on the right side of the road. Park you car here on the verge of the gravel road.

WHY?

The Finntorpsleden is a marked walk in a region called 'Finnskogen' ('the forests of the Finns'). Finnish nomads settled here in the 16th century and lived from what the forests and soil provided. The 'sights' (mostly overgrown remains) are less interesting than those of walk 3; but this is nevertheless a beautiful walk through the forests. In the spring and summer you can see lots of wild flowers and butterflies. The fact that the paths are so badly kept, makes one suspect that few hikers make use of this route. Therefore there is little chance of seeing other people; but the chance of seeing deer and other inhabitants of the forest, however, is more likely.

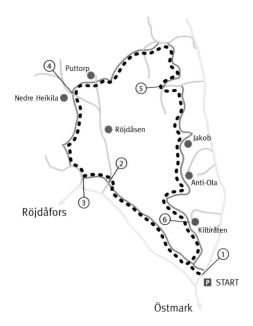

THE WALK

From the picnic table **(GPS1)** you cross the asphalt road. Head straight on, onto a sand road. The route is marked with orange paint. After 100 metres you head straight on, in the direction of 'Nedre Millomen'. Ignore all side-paths and follow the broad path. At a crossing with road signs (kraftverk/fotbolsplan) and orange markings you go straight on, towards a crossing with a gravel road and information sign **(GPS2)**. Cross the road straight ahead and continue along the narrow forest path, in the direction of 'Heikila'. After circa 75 metres go to the left. Follow the orange markings and the winding forest path until you reach a gravel road **(GPS3)**. Turn right, and after 200 metres, near a road sign and orange markings, right again. The path goes up. At the top, near the sign 'Kujaberg', you ignore an exit to the left to 'Jordkula' and turn right. Follow the narrow marked path. Ignore an orange marked exit to the left and follow the markings going straight ahead. Follow the path until you reach a gravel road, near a picnic table **(GPS4)**. Turn left here and then right just before the sign 'Heikila'. Ignore a path to the left and the sign 'Torplämning' ('remains'). Head straight on and follow the markings. The path bends to the right and becomes narrow. Ignore another exit ('Torplamning'). At a crossing you turn right and cross a field and go straight on. Follow the narrow path which goes around the house. You will reach a gravel road. Turn left. 10 metres further on, at the 'Puttorp' sign; you turn right, into the forest and the path descends. At the

'Pessaho' sign, you take a left turn and go past the sign 'Rackasomyren' and a shelter. You come to a broader gravel path. Turn left here and go right after 10 metres, into the forest. Continue following the orange markings until you reach a pasture with picnic table. Go left and after 30 metres you will reach a gravel road **(GPS5)**. Go right here. After 300 metres, you turn right and go into the forest at the orange marking. Follow the narrow, winding path which is sometimes heavily overgrown. Further on, the path is more visible. Ignore all side-paths and pass the remains of 'Sikasängen'. Just before the edge of the forest, near a house, the path goes to the right. Walk around the house. Further on, the path goes up. Ignore all side-paths and pass the 'Skinnarn' sign. Continue until you come to a crossing of gravel roads. Turn left and, after more than 300 metres, right at a crossing with another gravel road. Follow the bend to the left and 50 metres further on, at the orange marking, go left onto a forest path. Further on, you will walk along the edge of a stretch of cleared forest. Keep left where a signpost points to the right to 'Kolningsgrop'. Follow the orange markings through the open field. The path bends to the left and you will pass the sign 'Kling'. The path leads you through the forest. You will pass the sign 'Jakob'. Go straight on, at a crossing with a broad sand path, in the direction of 'Korpkullen'. At the edge of the forest you keep left. The path goes through the open field. Go passed the 'Antiola' sign and keep right on a broader grass path. Ignore a side-path and keep following the narrow path with orange markings. At a crossing with a broader, overgrown grass path, you turn right. Near a stretch of cleared forest you head straight on through the field. Keep left and walk back into the forest. Walk past the remains of 'Grentorp' and continue along the path. You will reach 'Kilbråten' **(GPS6)**. Keep to the right of the open area, along a wall of piled up rocks. Keep right at the edge of the forest and follow the markings. Further on, you turn left and near the electricity cables you go right. Ignore a path to the left ('Torplämning') and go straight on. Ignore a path to the right ('Jordkoja'). Turn right at the remains of a wooden cottage. Follow the orange markings and keep left. Turn left on a sand road at some signposts. Walk back to the asphalt road, the picnic table **(GPS1)** and your car.

GPS COORDINATES WALK 12 - ACROSS THE MOSSHÖJDEN AND ALONG LAKE BOVIGGEN

1. Red house (car)	N 60˚25.254 • E 12˚47.062	4. Gravel road	N 60˚25.893 • E 12˚48.903
2. Signpost with arrow	N 60˚24.801 • E 12˚48.158	5. Right into the forest	N 60.25.855 • E 12˚47.295
3. Gravel road	N 60˚25.530 • E 12˚49.101	6. Gravel road along the lake	N 60˚25.936 • E 12˚46.905

DISTANCE:	8.2 km
TYPE:	tour
TIME:	ca 3 hours
DIFFICULTY:	1

ÖSTMARK

Across the Mosshöjden and along Lake Boviggen

GETTING THERE

Östmark is situated northwest of Torsby. In Östmark you take a right turn to 'Kristineham 19'. After 4 km you will enter the hamlet of Metbäcken. After 1.7 km you take a left turn at the sign 'S Tvärberg 5' and follow this road for 11 km. You will first drive on an asphalt road, but further on this road becomes a gravel road. Ignore the side roads. When you see the lake on your left, you will also see a red house. Park your car here.

WHY?

Despite quite a lot of climbing at the beginning of this walk, in which you will cover about 200 metres of height difference, this is a relatively easy walk through a charming area. The owners of this forest have chosen to let nature run its course as much as possible. This is why the forest seems much more natural than elsewhere, where foresters have often left behind their marks. From the shores of Lake Boviggen you will gradually climb to the top of the Mosshöjden, from where you have a beautiful view. Here, you will also find a small hut where you can stay the night (also see www.boviggen.se). Towards the end of the walk, you will pass the remains of the Boviggen farm that was founded by Finnish immigrants in the early 17th century. Interestingly, their descendants lived at the farm until 1935.

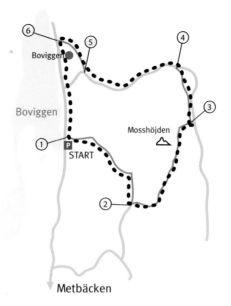

Boviggen

Boviggen

Mosshöjden

START

Metbäcken

THE WALK

Walk from the parking area, next to the red house **(GPS1)**, along the gravel road. After 100 metres you will see an information sign on your right. The route is marked with orange paint. Here you turn right, into the forest. After 50 metres you keep to the left. Follow the broad, ascending and overgrown path with orange markings. You ignore a path to the left twice. Further on, the path curves to the left; it becomes narrow and winds through the trees. The path continues to go upwards. The path turns to the left and ascends further. Just after that you take a right turn following the orange markings. The path slightly goes to the right. You will walk through a swampy, moss covered area and after some time you will reach the border of the old and new forest. Keep to your right. Ten metres further on the path goes to the left and you will walk through a newly planted area. On the left side of the path is a brook/gully. The path curves to the left and you will pass the brook via a duckboard. You will continue along the brook/gully and come to an orange sign post with an arrow **(GPS2)**. Take a left turn here and follow the path upwards. The broad path now runs through open terrain. Ignore a broad path to the left. You will pass a brook via a wooden duckboard and come to the front of a wooden cottage where you take a left turn and continue along the narrow path with the orange markings. You will now come through an area with lots of heath, across the ridge of the mountain. The highest point of this Mosshöjden is 525 metres. Keep following the winding path with the orange markings. Further on, the path undulates and you will walk through forest clearing, where the path is hardly visible. Pay close attention to the orange markings. Further on, the path descends even further. Follow the broad grass path between the newly planted area. You will then come to a gravel road (**GPS3**). Here you take a left turn and after 20 metres further on, at the orange marking at the left of the road, you go into the forest. Here too, the path is not always clearly visible. The orange markings indicate the direction. Follow the ridge of the hill; further on the path descends. You walk along the edge of a forest clearing. Halfway along, the path curves to the left into a field. Follow the orange markings through the terrain as closely as possible. You continue into the direction of a gravel road. Once you have reached the gravel road (**GPS4**), you turn left. Follow this road for about 1.600 metres until the orange markings, in a curve to the left, takes you to the right into the forest (**GPS5**). The path curves to the left and further on slightly to the right again. The path winds through the forest. Keep following the markings. You will pass a sign with information about the remains of the Boviggen farm. You will walk straight through part of the farm and see the remains of the walls in the grass. Further on, you will see a pile of rocks, after which the path will curve to the left. On the right you can see the remains of an ice cellar. Further on, you will come across another information sign with information about the farm that once stood here. Just beyond this sign you take a left turn downwards. Follow the orange marked narrow path until you come to the gravel road next to the lake (**GPS6**). Take a left turn here. Follow this gravel road for over one kilometre until you reach the red house (**GPS1**), where you have parked your car.

GPS COORDINATES WALK 13 - THE MOUNTAINS ALONG THE KLARÄLVEN RIVER

1. Sports centre	N 60°42.631 • E 12°53.138	5. Gravel road	N 60°42.897 • E 12°58.020
2. Y-crossing with post	N 60°42.935 • E 12°53.372	6. Shelter	N 60°41.869 • E 12°57.710
3. Gravel road + toilet building	N 60°43.583 • E 12°54.769	7. Gravel road	N 60°40.600 • E 12°57.481
4. Signs 'Biotop-skydd'	N 60°43.735 • E 12°55.876	8. Shed	N 60°42.536 • E 12°53.856

DISTANCE:	20.1 km
TYPE:	tour
TIME:	ca 6.5 hours
DIFFICULTY:	3 (distance, climbing/descending)

SYSSLEBÄCK

The mountains along the Klarälven River

GETTING THERE

Sysslebäck is situated on the through road from Torsby to Trysil. You will enter the village via the 62. Pay attention to the road signs that point you to the left, to the Simhall/Sports centre and Tourist Information. Turn off the road here and park your car in front of the sports centre.

WHY?

This brisk mountain walk is absolutely worth the effort! You will climb to a mountain-top three times and in total you will cover a difference in height of over 350 metres. On your way to the top and down again you have a stunning view of the valley of Klarälven River and the surrounding summits. You will walk across a part of the Nord-värmlandsleden, the regional long distance path. In the spring, the undisturbed nature is exuberant here, with all sorts of wild flowers and even orchids. The mountaintops are part of a huge unbroken area that continues into the neighbouring province, where you will hardly meet anyone. The perfect natural habitat for moose, bears and wolves.

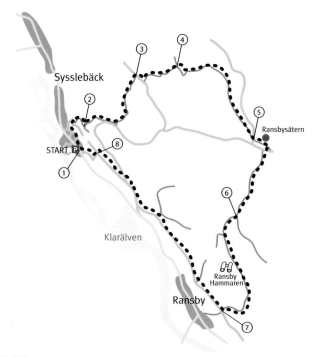

DE WANDELING

From the sports centre **(GPS1)** you walk back to the through road and cross it. From here you follow the marking of the Nord-Värmlandsleden, in the direction of Branäs-berget. The route is marked with orange paint. At the end of the road you turn left on the Kvistbergsvägen. After 150 metres, you turn diagonally to the right and follow the orange markings towards the electricity posts, via a narrow path between the trees. The path goes up and comes to a crossing. Here, you turn right and up, via a gravel road. Follow this with a bend to the right. After more than 100 metres, you take a sharp left turn, onto an ascending grass path. You will pass a picnic bench and the path winds up. At a Y-crossing near a wooden post **(GPS2)** you turn left. Follow the orange markings while the path goes up. At the crossing at the end of the path you turn left. At a crossing with the sign 'Kampisled' you go straight ahead. You now walk parallel to a gravel road. Via a wooden bridge you will cross a brook. Immediately after that, on a crossing of paths, you go straight on. Attention: from here you will no longer follow the route of the cross-country path (marked with ◆). The path goes to the left. Ignore a narrow path to the right. Keep following the orange markings, along the electricity wires, through the open field and further on into the forest again. Via duckboards you will pass a swamp-like area. Via a bridge you will cross a brook: Helsikebäcken. Follow the path until you reach a gravel road, near a toilet building **(GPS3)**. Turn right here, in the direction of Branäsberget. After 250 metres, the orange markings point you to the left, onto a broad ascending grass path. Further on, you will walk through a large stretch of cleared forest. Follow the path and go into the forest again, a little further on. You will now walk through a swampy area, and sometimes across duckboards. At a crossing of paths, near a post with the signs 'Biotop-skydd' **(GPS4)**, you turn right and follow the orange marking. Further on, the path bends to the left and goes down slightly towards a little valley. Continue along the path, which is now narrow and overgrown. Via a peat area you continue into the forest. You will pass a brook and the path goes up. Keep following the orange markings – sometimes you have to search for it – and you will reach a height of circa 500 metres above Amsterdam Ordnance Datum. On the highest point of the mountain, the trees have been cut down. Further on, you go into the forest again. After that you will again walk through a stretch of felled forest and on the right you can see a little lake. Follow the markings into the forest again. The path descends and you will come to a gravel road **(GPS5)**. Here you turn right and after 50 metres you go left and up, via a narrow path. Cross a brook and a swampy area via duckboards and continue until you reach a gravel road with road signs. Turn

left here to Ransby Sätern. After your visit to the Sätern, you go back via the gravel road. Turn left at the signpost for cross-country skiers.

Further on, you can see the orange markings again. Via a long duckboard you come to an open area and a gravel road. Turn right here and onto an ascending gravel road. Leave the markings of the cross-country path. After 150 metres, you go left at a crossing, onto a gravel road. In a curve to the right you take a narrow path on the left and go straight on, into the forest. You will partly walk across duckboards. The path winds up. Ignore side-paths. Keep following the orange markings until you reach the cleared mountain top. Follow the narrow path. Further on the path descends. You walk across a duckboard and reach a stretch of cleared forest. Cross a broad forestry path twice. Follow the orange markings and pass a swampy area via two duckboards. You will reach a shelter **(GPS6)** and a picnic bench. Head straight on and keep the cabin to your left.

You will walk across duckboards and jetties for some time. The broad path becomes narrow, curves left and runs besides a broader forestry path. After 100 metres, the narrow path crosses this broad path. Follow the orange markings along the ascending path that reaches a viewpoint: Ransby Hammaren (468 metres above Amsterdam Ordnance Datum). From here you can overlook Klarälven River. Keep following the path across the ridge. It goes down and up again further on. The path starts going down more steeply and you will walk through an area of newly planted trees and underneath electricity cables and into the forest. The path keeps descending and is sometimes rather steep. Follow the orange markings until you reach a gravel road **(GPS7)**. Turn right and keep following this road for about 3.5 km. Ignore side-roads and go on until the T-crossing at the end. Turn right here, direction Ransbysätern. At a Y-crossing you keep left, onto a descending path. Near a wooden house on the right, you turn left, before a shed **(GPS8)**. This gravel road becomes an asphalt road. The narrow road goes down and at the end it comes to the Sysslebäck through road. Turn right and take the first road left, the Badhusvägen. Continue on this for 100 metres until you reach the sports centre **(GPS1)** and your car.

GPS COORDINATES WALK 14 - THROUGH THE VALLEY OF KLARÄLVEN RIVER

1. Wärdshuset Spader2	N 60°43.993 • E 12°52.105	4. Bridge near Ransby	N 60°40.221 • E 12°56.513
2. T-crossing after bridge	N 60°43.810 • E 12°51.594	5. Gravel road	N 60°40.596 • E 12°57.467
3. Brook and waterfall	N 60°41.164 • E 12°54.800	6. Through road	N 60°42.549 • E 12°53.504

14

W A L K

DISTANCE: 10.0 or 18.8 km
TYPE: tour
TIME: ca 2.5 or 5 hours
DIFFICULTY: 1 or 2 (distance)

SYSSLEBÄCK
Through the valley of Klarälven River

GETTING THERE
Sysslebäck is an elongated village near the through road from Torsby to Trysil. You will enter the village via the 62. Drive on until you see restaurant/hotel Wärdshuset Spader2 on the right side of the road. You can park your car behind the building.

WHY?
During this route, you will follow the run of the Klarälven River. At some points you will be able to see the river from nearby, at other points when you climb the hills surrounding the valley the river disappears behind the pine forests. While under way, you will pass a beautiful waterfall and follow the river until the bridge near the village Ransby, where you can break off the route after 10 km. The bus service is not very frequent, so check in advance for departure times. The longer route takes you past quiet forestry roads, high above the river, which you can see shining in the distance. There are no cafés or restaurants along the route, but you will get the chance to get refreshments in Sysslebäck.

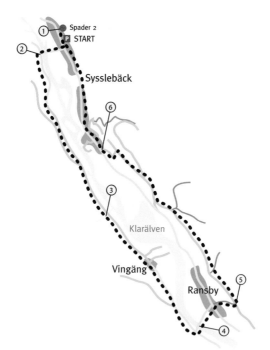

THE WALK

With your back to Wärdshuset Spader2 **(GPS1)** you turn left and walk along the through road for 100 metres. Take the first road on the right and walk towards the bridge across Klarälven River. Cross the river and ignore a path that runs left towards to river. At a T-crossing **(GPS2)** of asphalt roads you turn left. Follow the road for over one kilometre. Near a couple of houses you go straight on, onto the semi-paved road. Keep following this road which runs more or less parallel to the river. 6.7 km after the start, you will cross a broad brook with waterfall via a bridge **(GPS3)**. A little further on, you will walk through the hamlet Vingäng. After that the road becomes an asphalt road again. On your left you see the bridge **(GPS4)** across the river to Ransby. Walk towards it and cross Klarälven River again. After the bridge you walk straight on and ignore side-roads until you reach the through road. Cross this. If you want to break off the walk here (after 10 km), go to the bus stop on the right. A bus to Sysslebäck stops here a couple of times a day.

To continue the route, you cross the road and head on to the opposite unpaved path. From here you shortly follow the orange markings of the Nordvärmlands-leden. You will pass two houses and go straight on into the forest. The path goes to the right and up. At a Y-crossing you keep right and follow the marking. Pass a brook and keep following the ascending path. You will then come to a broader gravel road **(GPS5)**. Turn left here, and stop following the orange markings. Follow this path for about 3.5 km. Ignore side-roads and continue until the T-crossing at the end of this path. Here you turn right, in the direction of Ransbysätern. Keep left at a Y-crossing, a descending path. Near a wooden house on your right you turn left, along the front of a shed. This gravel road soon turns into asphalt. This narrow road descends and reaches the through road **(GPS6)** to Sysslebäck. Take a right turn here and take the first path to the left, the Badhusvägen. Go immediately to the right, into a dead-end street which will take you to the through road again. From here you follow the footpath along the road, in the direction of Sysslebäck centre. After circa 2.5 km you will reach Wärds-huset Spader2 **(GPS1)** where your car is parked.

Walking in Värmland

GPS COORDINATES WALK 15 - LÅNGBERGET, LAKE EGGSJÖN AND LAKE NORSKBROSJÖN

1. Parking space	N 60°49.119 • E 12°52.712	4. Bigger weir	N 60°51.404 • E 12°53.192
2. Crossing broad sand path	N 60°49.478 • E 12°53.701	5. Exit Långberget	N 60°50.201 • E 12°49.755
3. Crossing of asphalt roads	N 60°49.543 • E 12°55.366		

SYSSLEBÄCK
Långberget, Lake Eggsjön and Lake Norskbrosjön

GETTING THERE

From Sysslebäck you drive north along the river. Just outside the village there is an exit to the right, to Långberget. Take this exit and follow the signs to the Långberget Sporthotel. Park your car in the parking area, next to the lawn bowling alley, just before the hotel.

WHY?

This walk follows part of the 67 km long Nordvärmlandsleden, the long-distance path through the region. Outside the skiing season, the wintersport area of the Långberget is extremely suitable for beautiful walks. From the mountain you have stunning views of the surrounding hills. Part of the area is a protected area of natural beauty. There is a reasonable chance of seeing moose and there are also bears. If you do not see any of these wild animals, in the summer you will certainly get the chance to see the stray cattle of the Vålhallasätern. These animals are not at all shy and very curious. The shores of the Eggsjön and the Lake Norskbrosjön are excellent for a picnic.

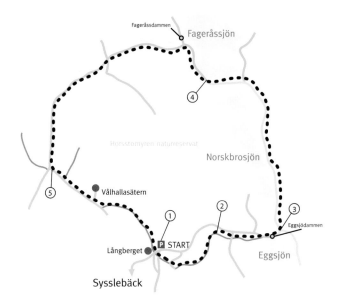

THE WALK

From the parking area **(GPS1)** you go up to the hotel. Walk around from the right. From here you follow the orange markings of the Nordvärmlandsleden. Just past a shed behind the hotel you go diagonally to the left and down. Via some steps you will pass a drain and on the crossing immediately after that you keep left. Further on, you will cross a duckboard. On a crossing with a finger post with a sign 'Hastbergssätern' you turn left. This path descends in a reasonably straight line. Take the first path that descends diagonally to the left, towards the lake. Keep following the orange marking. This path crosses a broad sand path **(GPS2)**. Go straight on here, onto a narrow path that descends between the trees. You will pass the foundations of some sort of a building and further on you come to a crossing with a wider path. Here you turn left. Just further on, you come to open ground and here you turn right. Keep left after that, in the direction of an asphalt road. On this road you turn right. Ignore an exit to the left. A little further on, you will reach Lake Eggsjön. Turn left here, across the weir along the shores of the lake. Just after a slight bend in the weir you turn sharply to the left, onto a descending path. You will also leave the orange markings here. At the bottom of the path, you turn right and continue until a crossing of asphalt roads **(GPS3)**. Go straight on here, in the direction of Lima. Keep following this road for quite some time. On your left you will see Lake Norskbrosjön. After a few kilometres, ignore an exit to the right and go straight on, in the direction of Fageråsdammen. From here, the road becomes semi-paved. You cross a little weir and further on a bigger weir **(GPS4)**. Before the Fageråsdammen you turn left, near a wooden shed and the sign Brattmon. Ignore two roads to the right and further on one to the left. After some time, you take the next exit to the left, in the direction Långberget **(GPS5)**. Just after this exit you can see a cabin on the right. Follow the orange markings again from here. Ignore side-paths and keep following the ascending road. Keep going until you see a blue finger post on your right which sends you to the left. From here, follow the narrow path between the trees. Along this path are also wooden posts with the orange markings. The path goes up. At a crossing of paths you go straight on, in the direction of Långberget. A little further on, you will pass some wooden cottages and keep following the path. Further on, the path goes through a pine forest and goes up. In some places you will walk across duckboards. You will come to a finger post and a cabin. Here you go diagonally to the left and up, in the direction of the Långberget Sporthotel. You cross an asphalt road and continue on the other side on the path with orange markings. Cross the asphalt road again and continue following the same path. You will come to a sand path between some holiday cottages. Cross this and go immediately diagonally to the right. Keep following the markings. The path bends to the left and finally reaches the Sporthotel, where your car is parked **(GPS1)**.

Walking in Värmland

GPS COORDINATES WALK 16 · THREE PEAKS

1. Building ski lift	N 60°10.255 • E 13°29.221	5. Broader path right	N 60°08.216 • E 13°31.068
2. Bend	N 60°09.498 • E 13°30.082	6. Highest point	N 60°09.022 • E 13°29.900
3. Crossing	N 60°09.169 • E 13°30.348	7. Crossing of paths	N 60°09.732 • E 13°29.287
4. Gravel road	N 60°08.798 • E 13°30.978		

DISTANCE:	9.5 km
TYPE:	tour
TIME:	ca 3 hours
DIFFICULTY:	2 (climbing/descending)

EKSHÄRAD

Three peaks

GETTING THERE

Ekshärad is situated about 25 km north of Hagfors, on the 62. Coming from the direction of Hagfors, you turn left at the crossroads in the centre of the village (near the supermarket ICA), in the direction Torsby. After about 1 km, you turn left at the sign that points to the sports facilities (ice hockey/ ski lift). You will reach a gravel terrain where you can park your car on the left, close to the ski lift building. **(GPS1)**.

WHY?

Ekshärad is a lively, small village, north of Hagfors. This liveliness is largely due to the fact that there is a fair chance of snow here in the winter, so that people can go skiing on the slopes of the Ekesberget. After the winter season, the walking season starts. That is why several walking routes have been set out. We describe the longest one here. This walk will take you to the top of this mountain and two other mountain peaks. Along the way, you will regularly get a good view of Klarälven River and Lake Mossbergsjön, especially when you walk through the area where the trees have been cleared. The paths are well-kept and the route is clearly marked.

THE WALK

Take the gravel road, before the ski lift building **(GPS1)**, to the left. Pay attention to the sign Vandringsled. You will follow the blue markings: 'Tre Toppar'. Near two sheds you take, on the right side of the road, a narrow path which runs across a field. Follow the blue-white markings and head straight on, past a natural water basin. At a crossing you go straight on, underneath the electricity cables. Go past the shooting range and straight on, onto a narrow path. The path curves to the right and you will reach a broader grass path. Go immediately left again. At the end you turn left on a crossing. Further on, this broad path bends to the right. You will reach a field and some houses. Follow the right side of the field here. Ignore side-paths and follow the bend **(GPS2)** to the left. After 50 metres, you turn right, onto a narrow forest path. After a while, at a crossing **(GPS3)** just before a picnic bench, you turn left. Follow the blue markings (white goes straight on). Ignore side-paths and follow the ascending path to the peak of the Norsberget. There you will find a shelter. The path descends. Ignore side-paths. You will reach a gravel road **(GPS4)**. Cross this and go onto the narrow blue-marked forest path. You will now reach a gravel road. Cross this too and carry on straight ahead across the (red and blue) broad forest path. Ignore side-paths until you reach a Y-crossing. Take the path on the right here, with the blue markings. Turn right at the next Y-crossing, onto a narrow path. After 50 metres, on a broader path, you turn right **(GPS5)**. You will reach a gravel road; go left and after 50 metres right, onto a grass path that goes into the forest. 50 metres further on you go right at a Y-crossing (blue markings). At the next Y-crossing you go right again, onto a narrow forest path. You will come to an area where the forest has been cleared for the most part. Further on, continue straight on, onto the narrow path and between the trees. This path leads to a cleared area. Follow the blue marking on the tree stumps. Further on, near one of the few trees that have not been cut down, you turn right and into the forest. At a crossing you turn left, on to an ascending path. The white markings joins the blue-white markings again from the right. Follow it upwards to the top of the L. Ekesberget. The path shortly follows the ridge and descends again after the highest point **(GPS6)**. Follow the blue-white markings. You will reach a broader path on the edge of the forest. Turn right and immediately left, going underneath the electricity cables. Follow the forest path and cross a broad path. Keep following the markings, even when the path goes up. Ignore side-paths. A climb will take you to just below the top, where the path goes slightly down and then up again. At a crossing of paths **(GPS7)** you turn right. Further on, you will pass a picnic bench and a lookout tower. After that the path descends. Follow the blue markings. Ignore side-paths. You will pass an electricity substation. Continue on the broad path and ignore the white markings that goes to the left. You will shortly follow the orange markings. At a Y-crossing you keep left. You will descend via a broad path. At the edge of the forest, before the ski lift, you descend. You now descend towards a broad path via the ski run. Here you turn right and further on you take the asphalt road. When this bends to the left, you head straight down the slope. You will reach the building of the ski lift **(GPS1)**, where your car is parked.

GPS COORDINATES WALK 17 · AROUND LAKE VÅGSJÖRNA

1. Red house along gravel road	N 59°48.554 • E 13°34.586	4. Wooden jetty	N 59°47.197 • E 13°33.018
2. Fryksdalskarolins Säter	N 59°47.968 • E 13°34.244	5. Edge of the lake	N 59°48.011 • E 13°33.506
3. Brook	N 59°47.565 • E 13°33.705		

MUNKFORS
Around Lake Vågsjörna

GETTING THERE

Munkfors is situated on the 62, the road from Karlstad to Hagfors. Take the exit Munkfors (roundabout) and go immediately right on the next roundabout. Follow the white signs 'Konferens Center' for 1.2 km. Immediately after the Konferens Center, you take the exit to the right, the O: a Hagetvagen. Follow this asphalt road which later becomes an unpaved road. After 600 metres you ignore an exit to the right. 2.2 km after the Konferens Center you turn right at a Y-crossing. 2.5 km further on, there is a red brown house on the right side of the road **(GPS1)**. You can park your car here.

WHY?

According to the marking, this beautiful walk is 8 km long, but according to our GPS it is only 7 km. Whatever it may be, it is an easy and pleasant walk around a lovely forest lake. It is wonderfully quiet and in the summer you can have a swim and picnic at the start and the end of the route. Along the way, you will walk across well-marked forest paths and you will be able to see all the shades of green that nature has to offer. If you want to continue the walk: at the same place the red marked Säterrundan starts, which is a walk of 4.2 km. Here we only describe the tour around Vågsjörna.

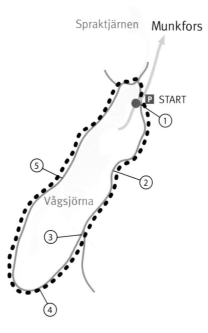

Spraktjärnen Munkfors

START

Vågsjörna

THE WALK

From the red house **(GPS1)** you walk to the picnic bench, in the direction of the lake. Turn left at the road sign 'Vagsjörund'. The route is marked green-white. Cross the gravel road a little further on and continue straight ahead onto a wide forest path. Keep right after 20 metres, onto a narrow path that leads into the forest. At a crossing with a wider path, you go left and up, and after 15 metres right again. You will cross a wider path. The path goes up and further on you will walk through a stretch of cleared forest. Head straight on there and follow the green-white markings. Further on, the path curves into the forest again and descends. You will then walk across more open terrain. Keep to the right. Go into the forest again and cross a brook. Further on, you will pass the remains of the Fryksdalskarolins Säter **(GPS2)**. Further on, you will walk across more open terrain again. In the distance you can see the lake. Pass a duckboard twice and keep following the narrow path with markings. On a gravel road you go straight on and after 10 metres you go right and into the forest again. You cross a brook via a bridge **(GPS3)**. The path ascends to the top of the hill, keep following the marking. Via a large wooden jetty **(GPS4)** you will pass an area of peat. After that the path will be peat-like. Further on, the path becomes a forest path again. You will pass a brook via a large jetty. Continue along the forest path and walk on until you reach a wooden house. Ignore the path to the right and continue straight on. Further on, the path ascends again and on the top it bends to the right. From here, the path winds through the forest and descends. Ignore side-paths and follow the green-white markings. You will reach the edge of the lake **(GPS5)**. Follow the path along the shores. Further on, you will pass a picnic area. Keep right at a crossing, going to a narrow path along the shore. You will pass a wooden shed and a little further on the path curves away from the lake again. At a crossing of narrow paths you turn right, onto a descending path. You will pass a brook. Further on, you will cross a long duckboard through a peat area. A little further on, you turn right at a crossing and cross a brook via a duckboard. You will see the red house. Walk diagonally to the left, towards the road where your car is parked **(GPS1)**.

GPS COORDINATES WALK 18 · JÄVERÖN ISLE

1. Ferry bridge	N 59°23.394 • E 13°39.744		5. Shelter	N 59°21.326 • E 13°37.912
2. Sign and signpost	N 59°22.828 • E 13°38.541		6. Both sides road signs	N 59°22.290 • E 13°39.335
3. Broad path	N 59°22.305 • E 13°37.937		7. Picnic bench	N 59°22.350 • E 13°40.102
4. Immediately left	N 59°21.636 • E 13°36.752		8. Left into the forest	N 59°22.835 • E 13°39.687

KARLSTAD
Jäverön Isle

GETTING THERE
From Karlstad, take the E18 in the direction of Stockholm. After about 10 km, you take the exit to Skattkärr. Then take the first road to the right, at the road sign 'Jäverön'. Drive down this road until the end, even when it becomes narrow and goes through the hamlet of Herrön. You will come to the little ferry that goes to the island. Leave your car behind on the right side and go on the ferry by foot. It takes off at 11:00 hrs.

WHY?
The best way to experience Lake Vänern is from one of the many islands which are 'off the coast' of Karlstad. Jäverön is a green oasis where only a few farmers live. Their connection with the outside world is the little ferry that sails here several times a day. Here, nature calls the shots. We saw deer, squirrels and many different kinds of birds. There even seem to be moose here! The walk takes you across the entire island and there are several places where you can interrupt your walk for a picnic or a dive in the cold water. If you continue walking at a quiet pace, you will be able to catch the boat back at 16:30 hrs. If you miss this, then the next (and last!) one leaves at 18:30 hrs. Upon arrival, always check the departure times.

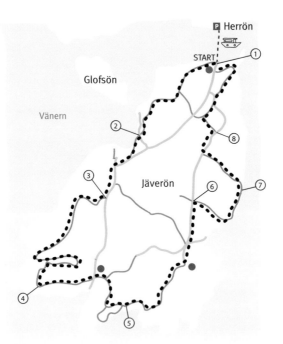

THE WALK

From the ferry bridge **(GPS1)** you follow the road up. After 20 metres, you go right, in the direction 'Smörhall'. The walk is marked with orange paint. Walk into the pasture and keep right, along the water. The path bends into the field. Follow the markings until the trees. There, you follow the left side of the field. Go through the fence and into the forest. At a crossing of paths (both marked orange) you go right. Follow the winding path, past the information sign 'Gammal Granskog', until you reach a sign and a signpost **(GPS2)** where you turn right. You will come to a gravel road. Go left and after 20 metres right, on to a narrow marked forest path. Climb across the fence and go past a picnic bench. The path goes straight on, across the rocks and after that into the field, in the direction of a shed. Via a fence you will reach a gravel road. Go right and at a crossing of paths left between sheds. Further on, a shorter route goes left. Go straight on here and continue the gravel road. At a road sign on your left, you turn right, onto a broad path **(GPS3)**. The orange marking is visible again further on. A bit further you go through the gate and immediately right, on to a narrow forest path. At a crossing near a signpost you turn left. Further on, you can go right towards a viewpoint. The route goes straight on. You will alternately walk through forest and across more open ground. Keep following the marking and go right at a road sign. On a broad path you go right and after 10 metres immediately to the left, on to a narrow path, past the fencing. Further on, you will cross a long duckboard. Just after that you go left, again passing fencing. At a road sign you turn right, on to an ascending path. 50 metres further on, you ignore an exit to the left, but continue along the path. Further onwards, the path is covered with rocks. Immediately after that you turn left **(GPS4)** (orange markings). Further up the path, you will cross a stretch of cleared forest. After that you go into the bushes again. Cross a gravel road straight on and keep left, going past a toilet cabin. Follow the gravel path. At a road sign you turn right, into the forest. At the sign 'Vindskydd & Grillplats 0.4 km' you turn right. At the shore of the lake you turn left. Further on, you will walk past a shelter **(GPS5)**. Follow the markings by the waterfront (painted on the rocks) until you reach a picnic bench. Choose the orange marked path that continues behind the picnic bench. Further on, you go right, on to a narrow twisting path. Keep following the markings. At a road sign you turn left. 50 metres further on, you go on towards a long duckboard. Shortly after that you turn left on a broader path and left again after 50 metres. Ignore side-roads and continue until you come to a crossing and a house. Turn left, onto a sand road. Where you can see road signs on both sides of the sand road **(GPS6)**, you turn right. After 0.8 km you will reach the shores of Lake Vänern. Here, you can choose between a forest path (Skogsstig) or a walk along the water (Strandpromenad). Both paths are marked, go past a cabin and further on, picnic bench **(GPS7)**. 100 metres after that, the paths bends inland. On a broader path you keep left; turn right after 10 metres. On a gravel road you turn right and after more than 400 metres you go left, following the orange markings into the forest **(GPS8)**. After 10 metres you keep to your right. At a crossing with an information sign you turn right. Cross the gravel road and keep to your left. Follow the forest path and go into the pasture by climbing over a fence. Follow the markings on the row of trees to the right. Further on, this bends to the left. Just ahead, you cross the field. On the other side you keep left. At the sign 'Strandskogen' you turn left and cross the field in the direction of a picnic bench. From here, follow the orange markings towards two sheds. Via a fence you will reach the gravel road. Turn right and walk towards the ferry bridge **(GPS1)**.

GPS COORDINATES WALK 19 - NATURE RESERVE LINSÖN PRÄSTÖN

1. Church Visnums-Kil	N 59°06.825 • E 14°03.337	4. Lookout tower	N 59°05.527 • E 14°05.018
2. Information sign	N 59°05.806 • E 14°03.859	5. Two wooden benches	N 59°05.047 • E 14°04.410
3. Crossing 'Björkholmen'	N 59°05.414 • E 14°04.324	6. Crossing 'Talluddarna'	N 59°05.391 • E 14°03.927

19 | WALK

DISTANCE: 5.5 or 10.0 km
TYPE: tour
TIME: ca 2 or 3 hours
DIFFICULTY: 1

KRISTINEHAMN

Nature reserve Linsön Prästön

GETTING THERE

From Kristinehamn, take the 26 in the direction of Mariestad. After 25 km you will reach a town called Nybble. Turn right at the petrol station. Follow this road for 7.6 km ignoring side-roads. At a crossing you go straight on to Visnums-Kil. Park your car after 100 metres on the right and off the road, in front of the church. For the short route you continue to the parking area as described at the start of the walk.

91

WHY?

Farmers had to make way for nature in this most southeastern part of Värmland. Since 1971, three small areas were given the status of Naturreservat (Nature Reserve). You can see for yourself how nature, slowly but surely, is getting the upper hand. What makes this walk special is that the route goes through deciduous forests, something quite unique in a landscape full of pines and spruces. The walk also takes you to the edge of the archipelago, the swampy strip on the shores of Lake Vänern, where many birds rest and brood. You will see lots of wildflowers and orchids and walk across narrow, overgrown paths. Long trousers are a necessity here.

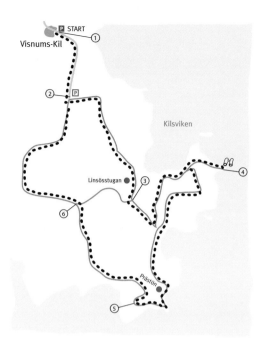

THE WALK

Follow the road past the church **(GPS1)**, which becomes a gravel road a little further on. After 200 metres, you will pass the old entrance gate of Nynäs. After 600 metres you turn right at the white sign post 'Linsön Prästön'. Follow this road for 1.4 km and ignoring a road to the right and left along the way. You will reach a parking area with an information sign **(GPS2)**. Continue along the gravel road past the sign. After 50 metres you turn left near a post with blue road signs: 'Vandringsled orange marking'. From here the walk is marked with orange paint. Go through a wooden gate and follow the narrow path that bends to the right further on. Further ahead, you will walk across some duckboards and in the direction of a wooden cottage, the Linsösstugan. Go through the fence and walk on the right side past the cottage. You will leave the grounds again on the other side via a fence. Pass a ditch via a duckboard and just further on you will pass a wooden shed near a brook. Continue the path across a little embankment. You will come to the crossing 'Björkholmen' **(GPS3)**. Here, you go straight on via a fence in the direction Prästön. You walk on along an overgrown grass path and a duckboard. At the sign 'Fågeltorn' you turn left, onto a narrow, overgrown path with orange markings. You will walk across a duckboard. Further on, you will be able to see the lake. Follow the path until you reach a small lookout tower **(GPS4)**. To continue the route you walk back 230 metres and turn left at the blue sign 'Fågeltorn', onto a path with orange markings. Via this narrow path you wind through the forest for quite some time. You will reach a crossing at the sign 'Prästön'. Turn left here and continue along the path. Keep left well before a shed. On the left you can see the big lake. Keep following the path and marking until you reach the edge of the forest. There are two wooden benches on the right **(GPS5)**. Turn right before the second bench going into the forest again. Turn left just before a derelict shed. A little further, you continue along the narrow path across an embankment. Follow the marking. You will pass a little fence and continue straight on, onto a grass path, along an open field. You will then reach a crossing 'Talluddarna' **(GPS6)**. Turn left and follow the marking through the field. Turn right at a crossing of grass paths. Pay attention to the marking. You will reach a fence at the edge of the forest. Go straight on here, along the edge of the forest. Cross the ditch via a duckboard. Further on, the path goes onto an embankment. Turn right at the end of the embankment, across a duckboard and further onto another embankment. Look out for an orange arrow on the tree. Follow the marking and keep left further on, going through the field. You will pass a duckboard twice and reach a fence. Go through the fence, across a duckboard and immediately left again. You will walk along the left side of the field. At the end, you go through a fence and straight on to the gravel road. You will reach the parking space with information sign **(GPS2)**. If you have chosen the shorter route then you will find your car here. For the longer route you continue along the road. Keep left at a Y-crossing and ignore a road to the right further on. At the crossing at the road sign 'Linsön Prästön', you turn left. Follow the road for another 600 metres until you reach the church of Visnums-Kil **(GPS1)**.

Walking in Värmland

GPS COORDINATES WALK 20 - THREE NATURE RESERVES NEAR BRATTFORS

1. Information sign	N 59°40.042 • E 14°01.336	6. Wooden bench	N 59°38.143 • E 13°56.397
2. Crossing with road signs	N 59°38.751 • E 14°00.835	7. Road sign to Brattfors	N 59°38.140 • E 13°57.336
3. Parking space 'Djupadalen'	N 59°37.992 • E 14°00.097	8. Crossing with road sign	N 59°39.195 • E 13°56.482
4. Road sign 'Gräshöjden'	N 59°36.568 • E 13°57.705	9. Road sign	N 59°39.241 • E 13°58.667
5. Asphalt road 63	N 59°37.394 • E 13°56.826		

20

DISTANCE:	20.7 km
TYPE:	tour
TIME:	ca 6 hours
DIFFICULTY:	3 (distance, climbing/descending)

WALK

FILIPSTAD

Drie natuurreservaten bij Brattfors

GETTING THERE

Coming from Karlstad, take the 63 to Filipstad. About 20 km before Filipstad, you will drive into Brattfors. 600 metres after the blue sign 'Brattfors', you turn right at the white sign 'Naturreservatet Lungälvs-ravinerna'. Take a sharp turn after 80 metres, on to a sand road. Park you car at the information sign on the lefthand side of the road.

95

WHY?

The longest and definitely one of the most beautiful walks in this guide. This route connects three protected nature reserves: Lungälvsravinerna, Geijersdalsmossen and Kittelfältet. The special landscape characteristics, like the river valley, the peat area and the craters, date back to the Ice Age. Between 1500 and 1920 these areas were used for forestry and the extraction of iron. The remains of this can still be seen near the old foundry and by the tracks of the former railway line, where horses pulled the loaded wooden wagons across the track. Nature in Lungälvsravinerna is exuberant and elsewhere there are also many different kinds of birds and plants. On wet days the subsoil in the ravine is very slippery. You will not be able to walk much faster than 2 km per hour on those days. This route takes almost an entire day.

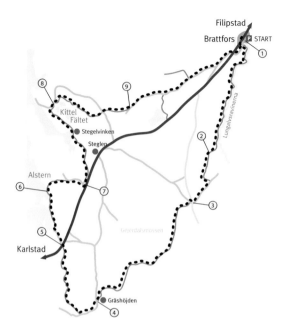

THE WALK

Facing the information sign **(GPS1)** you turn right. Just ahead is a wooden road sign with orange markings which you will follow the entire route. Follow the path along the through road. Cross the river via a bridge and go immediately to the left, in the direction of 'Lungälvsravinerna'. Follow the descending grass path. The path bends to the right. On a crossing, well before a shed, you go left. You will pass the sign '3 Dalen' where you go left and down some steps and a duckboard. Pass a brook via a little bridge. Follow the 2.5 km long path along the brook. You will regularly walk across duckboards. Continue following the orange markings and ignore side-paths. 3 km after the start you will reach a crossing with signs posts **(GPS2)**. Head straight on here, direction 'Djupa-dalen 1,8', across a duckboard and going up. Ignore any side-paths. On a crossing near a sign post you turn left, direction 'Djupadalen'. The path goes up and down again a couple of times. On a gravel road you turn right. Ignore side-paths. You will reach an asphalt road. Cross this diagonally to the right and go to the parking place 'Djupadalen' **(GPS3)**. Keep left and follow the orange markings, in the direction of Gräshöjden'. Follow the path across the ridge. On a crossing of paths you turn left, on to a straight path, later duckboard, which runs straight through the Geijers-dalsmossen. Near an informa-tion sign about this peat area you go right, on to a narrow path. You will now walk across an embankment, through the peat area. Follow the marking and walk across a duckboard again. On the next crossing you turn left. At a house and a road sign 'Gräshöjden' **(GPS4)** you turn right, direction 'Ångsågen'. After 30 metres, you turn right again. You cross a gravel road. On the next gravel road you head straight on, on to a narrow path. Follow this winding path for quite some time, up hill and down hill. Further on, the path goes straight through the forest, across the track of a former railway line. On a crossing with a gravel road, you go straight on, on to a narrow forest path. You will cross a broad asphalt road, the 63 **(GPS5)**. At the orange markings you go on to the forest path. Ignore side-paths until you reach parking space Ångsågen. Take the broad path right from the information sign, direction 'Brattfors 10.5'. Go right after 10 metres. Follow the orange markings, on to a narrow forest path. Go left near a road sign, towards the lake. There you go right, past a shelter. Follow the path along the lake. Further on, the path goes right and up and descends immediately after that. The path shortly follows the lake and then comes to a broad forest road. Turn left and after 10 metres, go straight on, on to a narrow forest path. Again, you will walk along the lake and after about 100 metres you go right at a crossing. The path goes up and past a wooden bench **(GPS6)**. Continue the path through the forest until you reach a gravel road. Cross this diagonally to the right and continue the path with orange markings. On a crossing with a road sign, you turn left towards 'Brattfors' **(GPS7)**. You will come to a crossing with road signs, go straight on here. Further on, you will go

past an open field and then into the forest again. You will walk across duckboards now and again. On a crossing with a road sign you go straight on.

Follow the markings until you reach the information pavilion 'Stegelvinken'. Go straight on here and keep the pavilion to the right. Follow the road sign 'Brattfors 7.3'. Cross a brook via a bridge and turn right after 15 metres. Near the lake the path bends to the left. At a crossing you head straight on. Ignore a path to the right and follow the broad path that goes through the forest. Turn right at a crossing. Ignore side-paths and at a crossing with a road sign **(GPS8)** you turn right, on to a narrow descending forest path. Just ahead, at a crossing of paths near a shelter, you turn left, towards Brattfors. Follow the marking. Keep right at the next road sign. Again, you will reach a crossing with a road sign. Go straight on. Further on, the path goes up. You will pass an information sign about 'Naturreservatet Kittelfältet'. At a crossing near a road sign you continue the path in the direction of Brattfors. Just after that you take the left path on a Y-crossing. Follow this path until you reach a gravel road. Go right here and after 10 metres left again, into the forest near the orange markings. When you reach a sand road you must take a right turn. Ignore a road to the right and go left after 50 metres, on to a narrow marked forest path. Follow this path for more than 1 km, continuing straight on. You will reach a sand road, near a road sign **(GPS9)**. Turn left here. On a Y-crossing you take the right path. On a crossing with a road sign to 'Stora Tjärn' you go straight on. After 150 metres, the orange marking sends you to the left, on to a narrow path, between the young pine trees. At a crossing with a broader path you go straight on. Keep left on a Y-crossing. Ignore side-paths and follow the marking. You will reach a gravel road. Turn right and at a crossing near a farm you turn left with the curve. Turn left at a crossing with an asphalt road and right at a T-crossing, in the direction of the main road. Cross this and go into the Hammarvägen. Ignore a road to the right. At the Y-crossing immediately after that you take the left road. When the road bends to the right, you keep left. Follow the path across the bridge and walk past the old iron foundry, back to the information sign **(GPS1)** and your car.

Walking in Värmland

1. Orange road sign	N 59°32.853 • E 14°17.445	5. Gravel road	N 59°33.988 • E 14°20.667
2. Gravel road	N 59°33.264 • E 14°18.992	6. Crossing with road sign	N 59°33.813 • E 14°19.576
3. Blue road signs	N 59°33.080 • E 14°19.765	7. Gravel road	N 59°34.339 • E 14°18.706
4. Crossing with road sign	N 59°33.266 • E 14°20.665	8. Gravel road	N 59°34.303 • E 14°17.674

21 WALK

DISTANCE:	11.9 km
TYPE:	tour
TIME:	ca 4 hours
DIFFICULTY:	2 (distance, climbing)

STORFORS

The forests around Lårhöjden

GETTING THERE

Storfors is situated on the 26, the road between Filipstad and Kristinehamn. From the direction Filipstad you take the exit to the right: Centrum/'I' (tourist information). Turn right immediately after that, in the direction of the Brand-museum and the tourist information office. Turn right just before that, via a viaduct underneath the 26. Follow the road in the direction of the camp site. Turn left before the railway line. Park you car at the side of the road, just past the entrance of the camp site, near the orange road sign.

WHY?

This is a nice forest walk through the outskirts of the province. You will alternately walk through a forest and peat area. In early summer the orchids are literally at the path edge and you will also see many different kinds flowers and butterflies. The first part of the walk is up a gradual climb to Lårhöjden, a beautiful spot for a picnic. You will not see many moose here, but we saw lots of squirrels in the area. This walk can be combined with a visit to the nearby Bjurbäcken stage lock, which is definitely worth a visit.

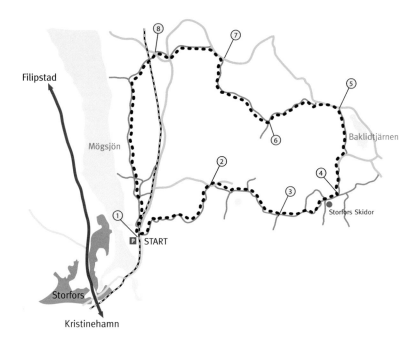

Filipstad

Mögsjön

Baklidtjärnen

Storfors Skidor

START

Storfors

Kristinehamn

THE WALK

At the orange road sign **(GPS1)** you walk into the field and cross a railway track a bit further on. On the gravel road you turn left and after 250 metres you go right, on to a narrow forest path. Ignore side-paths. Walk underneath the electricity wires and into the forest again. You will then pass a bridge and a duckboard. Follow the ascending path through the forest. Further on, the light green marking branches off. Keep following the orange markings and go straight on. You will walk across a duckboard again and further on you go up through a stretch of cleared forest. It is sometimes difficult to find the markings here. The path leads into the forest again. Follow the path until you reach a gravel road **(GPS2)**. Here, you turn right; the path goes up. After about 150 metres, you go right, on to a narrow path into the forest. You alternately walk across paths and duckboards. Ignore an exit to the right, towards a viewpoint. On a crossing of blue road signs **(GPS3)** you turn left, direction 'Lårhöjden'. Continue following path and markings. You will reach a cottage, Storfors Skidor. Walk left past the cottage. The path descends again and further on, at a crossing with road signs **(GPS4)**, you turn left. The path becomes a gravel road. Head straight on and ignore a gravel road to the right. Follow the descending gravel road. You will see in front of you the road sign 'Badplats 600 m' where the road turns to the right. Go to the left of the road sign and into the forest, on to a narrow, descending path. Continue this path until you reach a gravel road **(GPS5)**.

Turn left here. Follow the road and after 400 metres, go left at the orange markings on to a gravel path. Go right after 70 metres, into the forest via a narrow path. At a crossing near a road sign you turn left. Cross a little swamp via a small bridge. Follow the narrow path. You will have to walk on duckboards now and again. Keep to the left in a stretch of thinned out forest. Sometimes you will have to look for the orange markings here. Turn right on a crossing with a road sign **(GPS6)**. The path descends and further on, you will walk across a long duckboard that goes through a peat area. The path becomes a gravel road. In an open field you head straight on, on to a broad descending road. Ignore side-paths, the markings are missing sometimes. Choose the left path at a Y-crossing. 30 metres further on you turn left at a T-crossing with a gravel road **(GPS7)**. Walk underneath the electricity wires. After 50 metres, the orange markings send you left, on to a forest path. Keep right after 50 metres, going on to a forest path with a duckboard. The path goes up again and continues further on through, partly, open forest. Keep to the left at a sign post and keep right at the next one. You will reach a gravel road, which you cross straight ahead. Follow the marking. Cross another gravel road **(GPS8)** and go straight on, on to the narrow path. Head into the forest again and cross the railway track. Follow the path and orange markings until you reach a crossing with blue road signs and a picnic bench. Turn left, in the direction of 'Badsta Camping'. Ignore a road to the right (Utsikt) and continue along the path. At a crossing, choose the broader left path. Keep following this and ignore side-paths until you reach an orange road sign that sends you to the right. After about

100 metres you will reach a gravel road. Turn left here. Follow this road that bends to the right and ignore side-roads. You walk past a house and further on past the camp site. 100 metres after the road has turned into asphalt, you will reach your car at the orange road sign **(GPS1)**.

GPS COORDINATES WALK   22 - FORESTS AND PEAT AREA AROUND LAKE STOR-EN

1. Information sign	N 59°54.611 • E 13°27.846	6. Dolptorpet	N 59°55.469 • E 13°23.133
2. Little pool	N 59°54.293 • E 13°26.163	7. Gravel road	N 59°56.250 • E 13°25.024
3. Orange road sign	N 59°54.017 • E 13°25.392	8. Observation cabin	N 59°55.229 • E 13°26.127
4. Edge of forest	N 59°54.182 • E 13°23.927	9. Narrow path along lake	N 59°54.930 • E 13°26.434
5. Gravel road	N 59°54.692 • E 13°23.495		

22 WALK

DISTANCE: 15.6 km
TYPE: tour
TIME: ca 5.5 hours
DIFFICULTY: 2 (distance, badly kept paths)

MUNKFORS

Forests and peat area around Lake Stor-En

GETTING THERE

The starting point of this route is just north of Munkfors. Take the 62 from Munkfors to Hagfors. 8.1 km after Munkfors in Höje, take the left exit to V. Skymnäs. Pass the bridge and go left at the end of the road, in the direction of Munkerud. After 2 km, you turn right at a white sign that points to the Stor-En walk. After 1 km you go right again and after 2.1 km you go right once more. After 1.6 km you see a small information sign on your left. You can park your car here.

WHY?

The area in the triangle Sunne-Munkfors-Torsby has been moderately opened up as far as roads are concerned. The area is thinly populated, mainly because of the damp, peat-like subsoil which makes the area unsuitable for agriculture and habitation. As a result of this there is a great continuous area of forest, peat and swamp. The area has a great many wild animals and lots of special plants, like orchids and the relatively rare cloudberry, which is regarded a delicacy. Halfway into the walk, you can see that this area is best suitable for forestry. The past couple of years, quite a lot of trees were felled and this has left its marks on the landscape. The positive side is that various sorts of plants have started growing again and nature has received a new impulse and is now much more varied.

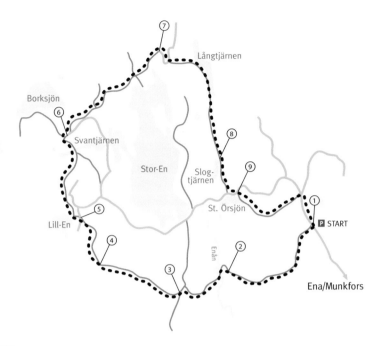

THE WALK

Facing the information sign **(GPS1)** you turn left, on to the broad gravel road. At the crossing immediately after that, you go straight on. Further on, you ignore a sand path to the right. The route is marked with orange paint; follow the orange paint the entire route. At the end of the gravel road you turn right, on to an overgrown cart track. The path goes up; ignore side-paths and keep following the markings. Further on, you walk underneath some electricity wires. The path becomes narrow and goes up again. Further on, you will walk through a stretch of cleared trees. After that the path descends to the right. Follow the path and the markings between the young trees. Further on, you enter the forest again. You wind through the forest and the path descends towards a little pool **(GPS2)**. Turn left here. Further on, you will walk through a peat area. On your right is a little lake. Cross a brook via a duckboard. Follow the path up. You will pass an observation cabin. On a Y-crossing of narrow paths you follow the left path. Ignore a narrow path to the left and follow the orange markings. After a steep descent, you can see a covered picnic area. Go left and up. Turn left at a crossing of orange marked paths. You will come to a broader path with a jetty. Go left here. 30 metres further on, you go right on a crossing. After 30 metres, an orange road sign **(GPS3)** points you to the right, on to a narrow path.

Further on, you will walk across a jetty through the peat area. After that, continue following the narrow forest path. You will reach another peat area, which you will cross straight on, partly via duckboards. You will now reach the forest edge **(GPS4)**. In front of you is a house. The route goes to the right here. Further on, the path goes across the border between forest and open field. Keep following the path and the markings, also along the edge of a peat area. You will reach an area of cleared trees. Follow the orange marking on the tree stumps. You will reach a gravel road **(GPS5)**, which you cross straight on. The path bends towards a lake. After this, keep right. You will shortly walk along the lake and after that the path again bends to the right. You will reach a crossing at the remains of Lillenstorpet (hardly visible). The orange markings go to both sides. Turn left here. The path bends to the right and goes up gradually. The foresters have caused quite some damage here. Follow the path and the orange markings as closely as possible. You will descend towards a little bridge across a stream that connects two lakes. Ignore the orange markings on your right. Cross the bridge and continue along the path. Follow the markings. You will reach the remains of Dolptorpet **(GPS6)**. Just before that there is a crossing. Again, the orange markings go both ways, but you turn right. After 150 metres, you will reach a gravel bank. Head straight on, onto a gravel road. After 50 metres you turn left at the orange

marking. Follow this through the field. Further on, you cross a brook via a duckboard. You alternately walk through stretches of forest and cleared trees. Ignore side-paths and follow the orange markings. You will reach an observation cabin. Further on, you will cross a peat area via a duckboard. On the other side, you go into the forest and up again. Further on is another duckboard through a peat area. You now walk past the peat area that borders Lake Stor-En. The path bends away from the lake and goes left further on. Cross a brook and go between the young trees. You will now reach a broad forestry path. Here, you follow the orange markings to the left. You will then reach a gravel road **(GPS7)**. Turn right here and after a bend to the left, the orange markings will send you right, on to a narrow forest path. The path descends. You will cross a peat area via a duckboard. At the end of the duckboard you go straight on. Further on, you will pass another duckboard. The path bends to the right and the left. There is a lake in front of you. The path runs along the right side of the lake. You will pass an observation cabin. Again, you will walk through a stretch of cleared forest. Continue following the marking, going straight on. After about 1.5 km you will reach the shores of a lake. Follow the path along the left side of the lake and pass another observation cabin **(GPS8)**. Cross a brook via a metal plank. Follow the path and marking. You will reach a gravel road by a lake. Turn left here. After 100 metres you turn right, onto a narrow path along the lake **(GPS9)**. There are hardly any markings here. Follow the path towards the end of the lake and cross a broad forestry road. Continue straight on and you will see the markings again. After 50 metres, you turn left onto a narrow orange-marked forestry path. This path descends and further on you turn left. The path goes through the forest. Keep left at a crossing and further on you keep right again. Cross a brook and follow the overgrown path. After a few hundred metres you will reach a gravel road. Turn left here. Ignore a gravel road to the left and after 400 metres you will reach the information sign **(GPS1)** where your car is parked.

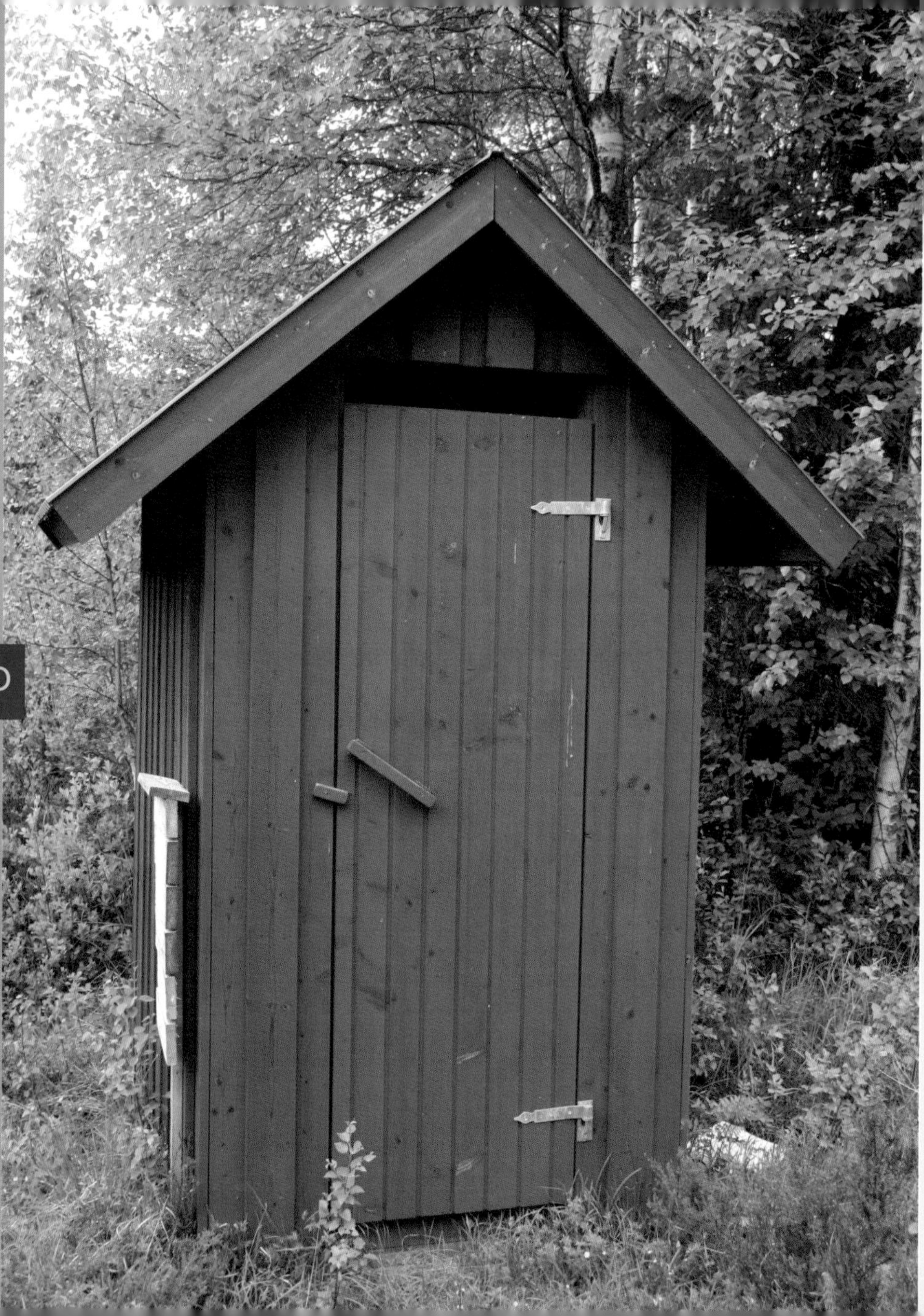

JUSTIFICATION

The authors of this book have walked and described all routes in this book during the spring of 2008. We have collected almost all routes through the local tourist information offices and via maps published by the Landmäteriet, the Swedish topographical service.

- Walks (7 and 9) through the Glaskogen Naturreservat are based on the general map published by park management.
- Walk 12 is based on a publication by Boviggen Verlag.

All photographs were made by the authors during their stay in Värmland.

Copyright is applicable to all itineraries, maps and photos in this guide (see also the imprint on the inside of the cover).

WE WOULD LIKE TO THANK

The owners of the four companies that have accommodated us during our stay in the region:

- Guesthouse Eleven, Brenda & Michel Muys, Arvika, www.elevenarvika.se.
- Storängens Camping, Marian & Patrick Zwier, Ransäter/Munkfors, www.storangenscamping.com.
- Stuvettsgard, Anky van Etten & Sylvia Stuiver, Gräsmark, www.stuvettsgard.se.
- Wärdshuset Spader2, Andreas Falke & Pieter Mans, Sysslebäck, www.spader2.se.

UPDATES OF THE ROUTES

All specifications have been carefully worked out and checked. Landscapes, however, are always subject to change. Therefore, it is possible that during one of the walks you will come across obstacles that we did not encounter when describing the route.

We would appreciate it if you could notify us about any changes and obstacles in the routes. Also welcome are suggestions for alternative routes. Please email your experiences to info@onedaywalks.com. We will make sure that all alterations can be consulted via the website. People that buy the book later, can check before departure if there are any additions or alterations in the itineraries.

Go to **www.onedaywalks.com/EN/Varmland** for the latest updates and alterations in the routes described.

Walking in Värmland